SYLVIA BROWNE'S
Book of Angels

Also by Sylvia Browne

BOOKS/CARD DECK

Adventures of a Psychic (with Antoinette May)

Astrology Through a Psychic's Eyes

Blessings from the Other Side

Contacting Your Spirit Guide (book and CD)

Conversations with the Other Side

Heart and Soul card deck

A Journal of Love and Healing (with Nancy Dufresne)

Life on the Other Side

Meditations

Mother God

The Other Side and Back (with Lindsay Harrison)

Past Lives, Future Healing

Prayers

Sylvia Browne's Book of Dreams

and . . .

My Life with Sylvia Browne
(by Sylvia's son, Chris Dufresne)

The Journey of the Soul *Series*
(available individually or in a boxed set)

God, Creation, and Tools for Life (Book 1)

Soul's Perfection (Book 2)

The Nature of Good and Evil (Book 3)

AUDIO PROGRAMS

Angels and Spirit Guides (also available as a CD program)

Healing Your Body, Mind, and Soul

Life on the Other Side (audio book)

Making Contact with the Other Side

Meditations (also available as a CD program)

The Other Side of Life

Prayers (also available as a CD program)

Sylvia Browne's Book of Angels
(abridged audio book/CD program)

Sylvia Browne's Tools for Life
(also available as a CD program)

and . . . *The Sylvia Browne Newsletter* (bimonthly)

(All of the above titles—except the newsletter—are available at your local bookstore, or by calling Hay House at 760-431-7695 or 800-654-5126.)

Sylvia Browne's
Book of Angels

HAY HOUSE, INC.
Carlsbad, California
London • Sydney • Johannesburg
Vancouver • Hong Kong

Published and distributed in the United States by: Hay House, Inc., P.O. Box 5100, Carlsbad, CA 92018-5100 • *Phone:* (760) 431-7695 or (800) 654-5126 • *Fax:* (760) 431-6948 or (800) 650-5115 • www.hayhouse.com • **Published and distributed in Australia by:** Hay House Australia Pty. Ltd., 18/36 Ralph St., Alexandria NSW 2015 • *Phone:* 612-9669-4299 • *Fax:* 612-9669-4144 • www.hayhouse.com.au • **Published and distributed in the United Kingdom by:** Hay House UK, Ltd. • Unit 62, Canalot Studios • 222 Kensal Rd., London W10 5BN • *Phone:* 44-20-8962-1230 • *Fax:* 44-20-8962-1239 • www.hayhouse.co.uk • **Published and distributed in the Republic of South Africa by:** Hay House SA (Pty), Ltd., P.O. Box 990, Witkoppen 2068 • *Phone/Fax:* 2711-7012233 • orders@psdprom.co.za • **Distributed in Canada by:** Raincoast • 9050 Shaughnessy St., Vancouver, B.C. V6P 6E5 • *Phone:* (604) 323-7100 • *Fax:* (604) 323-2600

Editorial supervision: Jill Kramer • *Freelance project editor:* Gail Fink
Design: Jenny Richards • *Interior illustrations:* Christina Simonds

Library of Congress Cataloging-in-Publication Data

Browne, Sylvia.
Sylvia Browne's book of angels / Sylvia Browne.
   p. cm.
ISBN 1-40190-084-4 (hardcover) • ISBN 1-40190-193-X (tradepaper)
   1. Angels—Miscellanea. I. Title: Book of angels. II. Title.
BF1999 .B716 2003
291.2'15—dc21
                                                              2002009339

Hardcover ISBN: 1-4019-0084-4
Tradepaper ISBN: 1-4019-0193-X

07 06 05 04   7 6 5 4
1st printing, April 2003
4th printing, April 2004

Printed in the United States of America

*To Reid Tracy and Daniel Levin . . .
not because they work for Hay House, but because they
have been more than friends in every way, and I want
to thank them for seeing me through many rough
times when they didn't have to.*

Contents

Author's Note

EVER SINCE I was a little girl, I've been fascinated and curious about the whole premise of angels. Do they exist? Did the holy cards the nuns gave me portray their appearance accurately? Do we become angels when we die?

Having been a Catholic at one time, I guess you could say I've always been partial to angels. Maybe it began with a prayer I learned as a small child:

> *Angel of God, my guardian dear,*
> *to whom God's love commits me here.*
> *Ever this day be at my side,*
> *to light and guard, and rule and guide.*

My interest in angels certainly continued throughout my Lutheran-Jewish-Episcopalian upbringing. (Didn't I say I was Catholic? I was, but first I was Lutheran, Jewish, and Episcopalian—I started life as a walking theological study in progress.) Over the years, my curiosity about angels was compounded by two things even greater than childhood prayers and Sunday-school stories. First, for as long as I can remember, my spirit guides have constantly referred to these heavenly beings. And second, in my work as a psychic, countless numbers of people have told me about their near-death experiences, astral projections, or even past-life regressions that included these beautiful beings of light who would guide these individuals, meet them, and stand at their bedsides.

For those of you who have read one or more of my books, what I'm about to tell you may be a bit redundant, but for those of you who are preparing to read one of my books for the first time, a little background is in order. As you may know, I'm a psychic and trance medium with clairvoyant and clairaudient abilities. I was born in 1936 in Kansas City, Missouri, with these abilities, and have never consciously known a day in which my God-given talents have not manifested themselves in one way or another. I don't know what it's like to *not* be psychic.

One of my psychic gifts includes the ability to communicate with my spirit guides, those beings from the Other Side who watch over me and help me live my life here on Earth. Every one of us has at least one spirit guide, maybe more. My primary spirit guide is Iena, an Aztec-Inca woman whom I affectionately named "Francine" the first time she spoke to me—when I was seven years old and couldn't pronounce her name right. She's been with me my entire life, and nobody could have a better friend.

I also have a guide named Raheim, from India, who spent his last life as a spiritual teacher. Using me as a trance medium (meaning that they use my body and voice to communicate to others while I'm unaware of what's being said), these two guides have conveyed countless hours of information to me that now make up a considerable research library of knowledge from the Other Side.

I can't and don't take credit for my abilities, for God made me this way. I've had my abilities tested time and again by doctors and scientists who come away amazed, but frankly, I'm my own worst critic and will be the first to tell you that I'm not 100 percent accurate—no psychic is or could be. In fact, at one time during my youth, I questioned my abilities and wondered whether I was mentally ill. After countless hours of self-doubt and consultations with psychologists and psychiatrists (they always said I was normal, with a high degree of paranormal ability thrown in), I just capitulated and went on living my life, using my psychic gifts to do good for others, devoting my life to that purpose, and trying to be as "normal" as possible. I'm beginning to think I've accomplished that last part, as I get thousands of letters and meet hundreds of people who constantly thank me for my work and for being "just folks." To me, that's the highest of compliments.

Now, after more than 60 years of being psychic, more than 40 years of research throughout which angels constantly reared their heads, and more than 20 years of comprehensive study into the subject of angels, I'm happy to bring forth *Sylvia Browne's Book of Angels*. Although I touched on the subject in some of my earlier work, this book includes even more definitive research into the description, colors, totems, and functions of angels, as well as new information about two additional levels, or *phyla,* of angels whose existence was previously unknown. I truly believe that anyone who reads this book will find many questions answered and many misconceptions about angels made clear.

In the pages that follow, you'll not only discover that angels are real, but also—through actual research and documented stories—how they operate and what they can do. This book is a compilation of academic study, as well as information delivered by Francine in a series of six weekly research trances. It was almost miraculous that, after each of Francine's trance sessions, a huge stack of angel stories would come into my office, almost telepathically relating to the specific phylum of angels we'd discussed the week before.

People scoff, but you can't tell me that there isn't a spiritual network in this world that resonates to truth. It's as if a message goes out into the atmosphere, and the angels in attendance pick it up and implant it into the minds of their human charges, many of whom say they felt compelled to write. In the following chapters, you'll get to read quite a few of those stories. I wish I could have included every word of every letter, but that would require a much bigger book than this one! Although the letters have been edited and the names have been changed to pro-tect the writers' privacy, I want to acknowledge each and every one of you who took the time to share your stories. You contributed immensely to my knowledge of angels and to the making of this book, and I will be forever grate-ful. Angels have always wanted their messages heard. Now, with God's help and yours, they have a voice.

As we travel down the path of life, we don't have to yearn in vain for companions along the way—we already have them. In all my years of theological research into the other dimensions, I've discovered an amazing thing: Not only does a belief in angels make perfect sense, but the feeling of truth and peace it brings is a sign that we've been touched somewhere deep inside, a sign that we *know* they exist. My friend Taylor who works at Microsoft has said that when I tell her something that feels right to her, she gets a chill. I call it the "psychic chill of truth." I've had chills many times while writing this book. I've felt the presence of angels more fully than ever before, and several times I was even aware of the slight rustle of wings. It seemed that the angels were, for lack of better words, eager or elated to get their information out. Even though angels don't experience human emotions like we do, I can't help but feel that they rejoice in our knowing who they are and what they can do for us.

For my "veteran" readers, welcome again, and a blessed thank you for your continued love and support. To my new readers, may your spiritual path and especially your knowledge of angels be augmented by this labor of love. I do hope you enjoy reading this book as much as I've enjoyed writing it, and I hope you'll use the meditations at the end of each chapter to call upon the angels to enfold you in their caring wings. May all of your angels gather around you every day to help you in your life . . . for they are always there . . . just as God is.

God love you, I do,

— **Sylvia**

Christina Simonds 2002 ©

I

Why I Believe in Angels

"Then I looked and heard the voices of angels around the throne and the living creatures and the elders, and the number of them was myriads, and thousands of thousands."

— Revelation 5:11

NOT ONLY have *I* never repeated the following story to anyone, but it has been *told* to only a few people, including my sister and me. My grandmother, Ada Coil, a great and well-known psychic in my hometown of Kansas City, Missouri, related it to me, and it was later validated by my mother; by a woman named Katherine; and by Bishop Spencer, an esteemed bishop in the Episcopalian church.

My grandmother had three children: Marcus Coil, her oldest son; Celeste Coil, my mother; and Paul Coil, the youngest son, who had Grandma's gift of psychic ability. Paul had a tremendous love of God, heard voices, and relayed messages to people. At the age of 20, he had a contract to sing at the WDAF radio station in Kansas City—and he also loved sports.

Paul had lettered in track and field and had won medal after medal in pole vaulting. He was 6'6" tall and lean, with huge brown eyes. One day he felt a small pea-like lump on his thigh. A doctor looked at it and at first waved it away. However, the lump started to grow, and the doctors began to take notice. Remember, this was 1930, and the medical profession, while improving all the time, was certainly not as advanced as it is today. Finally, at age 21, Paul was diagnosed with cancer.

The surgeons literally gutted his leg, but despite their efforts, they knew that Paul was going to die. Katherine, his fiancée, was inconsolable, and my grandmother wouldn't talk about it (until I came along in 1936, everyone said). Right before Paul died, he not only showed his psychic ability, but also the vision that was yet to come. Paul told my mother that she would have a daughter with large brown eyes who would have the "gift." He wanted my mother to name her Sylvia, after the title of one of his favorite songs.

On the day that everyone gathered—Bishop Spencer, Katherine, Mom, and Grandma—Paul was struggling for his last breaths. My grandmother was holding his hand when she said that he looked beyond her with a beatific expression she could never describe. Just then, the room filled with light. Even Bishop Spencer fell to his knees. Grandma said that complete peace and joy filled the room, and Paul told her, "Mother, this is an angel, and it has come for me."

Grandma said she felt rooted, not from pain, but from power and love. Paul, who couldn't move, suddenly raised himself up and tried to get out of bed. At that moment, a nurse burst through the door, Paul fell backward, the light went out, and the room grew dismal and cold.

Right before he died, Paul looked at Grandma and said that he knew his dad was in the same hospital, two floors below, with blood poisoning. No one had told

Paul about Grandpa for fear of upsetting him. Paul then looked at Grandma and said, "Dad will be over soon, the angel told me, and I will take care of him for you, Mom," and then he died. Grandpa Marcus died two weeks later, as Paul had foretold.

As Grandma later put it, although she'd lost a husband and a son, out of this immense pain she was, blessedly, privy to a visit from an angel.

Angels Appear in Every Religion

Although I've always believed in angels, I've usually been more inclined to call on my spirit guides for help or advice—that is, until about 20 years ago when I began to take a hard look at the stories and research. It was then that I started getting hooked on angels. In studying what the various religions had to say about them, I discovered that, through the morass of dogma from every corner of the spiritual world, angels have always held their own.

There's no religion (at least among the major ones) that doesn't contain some reference to these celestial beings. They seem to be above scrutiny, uniting all religions in a universal belief. Greek, Egyptian, and Roman mythology feature an assortment of winged creatures, including the gods Zeus, Jupiter, Horus, and Mercury. Wicca and pagan groups are given to a belief in angels and use them frequently as messengers to carry out certain functions. Even among the most hardcore agnostics and atheists, there seems to be a belief in angels, a fact that should cause even the most scientific-minded person to sit up and take notice. Something is obviously operating on a superconscious or subconscious truth level that resonates with the comforting, sometimes silent, knowledge that indeed, angels do exist.

Religious writings are filled with references to angels. The Bible alone contains approximately 600 such references. The Douay version, an English translation of the Latin Vulgate, indicates that the number of angels must be very large (3 Kings 22:19, Matthew 26:53, Hebrews 12:22), that their strength must be great (Psalms 103:20, Revelation 8:1-13), and that their appearance varies according to circumstances but is often brilliant and dazzling (Matthew 28:2-7, Revelation 10:1-2).

Mark 13:27 says: "And then He will send forth His angels and will gather together His elect from the four winds, from the farthest end of the earth to the farthest end of heaven," showing that God can call the angels up at will to help Him protect His precious children.

The Catholic Encyclopedia says that the word *angels* is derived from the Latin *angelus* and the Greek *angelos*, meaning "one going" or "one sent."

In *Ask the Rabbi,* written by Louis Jacobs and researched at the Ohr Somayach Institution in Jerusalem, the rabbi writes: "The Hebrew word for angel is *malach,* which means messenger. According to traditional Jewish sources, angels are the powers which fulfill the will of God."

In Hinduism, in the Bhagavad Gita (11.5), the Supreme Lord is talking to Arjuna (man and God are speaking). The Supreme Lord says, "Oh, Arjuna, behold my hundreds and thousands of multifarious divine forms that come in different colors and shapes."

In *Selections from the Writing of the Báb,* the great Baha'i messenger from God writes: "O Lord! Assist those who have renounced all else but Thee, and grant them a mighty victory. Send down upon them, O Lord, the concourse of the angels in heaven and earth and all that is in between."

Many historians, on writing about the life of Buddha, report that his first sermon was preached to many devas and Brahmas (angels and gods).

The Islamic faith depicts angels as unseen beings of a luminous and spiritual substance who act as intermediaries between God and the visible world. Belief in their existence enters into the Islamic definition of faith itself: "The Messenger believeth in what hath been revealed to him from his Lord, as do the men of faith. Each one (of them) believeth in Allah, His angels, His books, and His Messengers" (*The Meaning of the Holy Qu'ran* 2:285).

Besides the supreme beings, Zoroastrianism describes many classes of spiritual beings also known as *arda fravash* (holy guardian angels). Each person is accompanied by a guardian angel who acts as a guide throughout life.

John Neihardt, author of *Black Elk Speaks,* tells us that even the American Indian tradition speaks of angels. Black Elk, a holy man of the Oglala Sioux, said, "I looked up at the clouds and two men were coming. There headfirst like arrows slanting down, and as they came, they sang a sacred song, and the thunder was like drumming. 'Behold a sacred voice is calling you, all over the sky a sacred voice is calling.'"

As you'll learn in a later chapter, this sounds similar to what Francine tells us about the Cherubim and Seraphim: Their voices not only fill the sky, but fill our hearts and souls as well.

Angels and the Arts

When I began researching the subject of angels, the volume of literature I found myself swamped with was something not even a psychic could have predicted. Authors, artists, and poets too numerous to mention make no veiled attempt to hide their belief in the power and glory of angels. Not just religious writings, but literature, music, paintings, and mosaics abound with their images.

Most of us have seen the famous picture of the guardian angel helping children across what seems to be a precarious bridge; I know Catholic schoolchildren have seen this picture many times. And millions of people have traveled from all over the world to see Michelangelo's angels in the Sistine Chapel.

Angels turn up in numerous works of poetry and prose, from Edgar Allen Poe to one of my favorites, Henry Wadsworth Longfellow. Longfellow wrote: "As if with unseen wings, an angel touched its quivering strings; and whispers, in its song, 'Where hast thou stayed so long?'"

In "Hymn to the Beautiful," Richard Henry Stoddard wrote: "Around our pillows golden ladders rise, And up and down the skies with winged sandals shod, The angels come, and go, the Messengers of God."

In "A Cradle Hymn," Isaac Watts wrote: "Hush, my dear, lie still and slumber! Holy angels guard thy bed! Heavenly blessings without number gently falling on thy head."

In literature, Ralph Waldo Emerson told us: "So it is in rugged crises, in unweariable endurance, and in aims which put sympathy out of question, that the angel is shown."

Mary Baker Eddy, the founder of the Christian Science movement, described angels in this way: "They are celestial visitants, flying on spiritual, not material, pinions. Angels are pure thoughts of God, winged with Truth and Love, no matter what their individualism may be."

It's quite a journey when we go in search of angels. Whatever source we consider—Biblical, literary, or artistic—angels are alive throughout much of our past and present. Whether adorned with wings, halos, or harps, angels are always given the attributes of healing, solace, and protection. They've survived throughout the annals of time to tell us a very pointed truth: that they are loving and real, and they come from a God who will always take care of us.

Modern-Day Angels

Angels aren't relegated to just the classics and religious teachings. Lately they've been turning up on TV and in the movies, too. Of course, they've always appeared in "holiday classics" such as *It's a Wonderful Life* and *The Bishop's Wife,* but they were rarely seen in mainstream programming. Eventually, scriptwriters took some tentative steps into the supernatural with the TV show *Bewitched.* Then angels popped up occasionally on series such as *Little House on the Prairie.* Later, they gained top billing in *Highway to Heaven,* and today there's *Touched by an Angel,* a popular program that's held its own in the ratings since it first hit the airwaves. The movie *Michael,* starring John Travolta, was a little raw in terms of how it portrayed angels, but nevertheless, it marked the beginning of their imprint on human consciousness. Art imitates life, as they say, but art also imitates truth.

Over the last ten years, angels have penetrated the deepest consciousness of humankind. In fact, they're mentioned often in a variety of books, and are depicted in different forms in gift and specialty shops. Where angels once were relegated to places of worship, now we see cherubic angels with laurel wreaths on our mantels (as in my home); on lapel pins; and even tattooed on arms, legs, and (ahem) private parts. Why? My take is fairly simple. As I've stated many times in my lectures, so much has failed humanity that the world has turned to a higher spiritual belief, a gentler belief. And what could be more gentle than an angel?

Naysayers will argue that angels are just another metaphysical fantasy to relieve our minds and give us a false sense of security. If that were true, then why have they shown up in every religion and every form of art and literature, as well as being alive and well in the media? How could all these people, separated by geography, time, and culture, come up with the same knowledge or truth of these amazing beings sent by God?

I think the sudden resurgence of angels is also in direct rebuttal to the hellfire and demons we've had to put up with from so many religions. The angels, as I see it, have come into prominence out of our need to believe in an all-loving God, perfect in every way, who looks after His creations. Angels walk with us every moment of our lives. These beautiful beings, with light shining around them and wings spread out for protection, bring us not only the feeling and knowledge that we're not alone, but a certain freedom from worry. Over my mantel hangs a beautiful Campanelli painting of an angel with a hummingbird. Every time I look at it, it gives me peace and comfort. I know angels can't prevent all harm or keep us from lessons learned, but they certainly do create what we know or feel to be miracles here on Earth—very real pointers in life to show us that God listens, watches, and cares.

Make no mistake—angels are real beings, created and sent by God to aid humankind and serve as go-betweens for us and the Other Side. Angels are true messengers from God. In my mind's eye, I love the vision of an angel or angels going to God or to our life's chart (our "blueprint" for this life, which we wrote before we were born) and bringing back the answers to our most troubling questions. No matter how lonely or despondent we feel, we're definitely not alone. Angels are forever, and are always in attendance. Unlike some human beings, angels will never fail us, never be in a bad mood, and never get disgusted with us. They're direct reports from God, always in a state of acceptance and unconditional love.

New Information about Angels

Seventeen years ago, I founded a Gnostic Christian church called the Society of Novus Spiritus (New Spirit). Whether you call us Essenes, Knight's Templars, or Cathars, we are the oldest religion, the religion practiced by Christ. We seek, search, and probe until we find the truth, and that is why we say, as Christ did: "Seek and ye shall find. Knock and it shall be opened unto you." The greatest thing about our Gnostic religion is that it stays pure and keeps advancing with more and more extensive knowledge. Our Gnostic theological process is the same that was used to gain knowledge on the Other Side: We gradually accumulate more information as we go along, finding the answers to questions heretofore classified as mysteries.

As a Gnostic Christian, I've done my own extensive research, but my spirit guide Francine has always provided more specific details. For 40-some-odd years, she's relayed material and prophecies way ahead of our time. Not long ago, Francine held a series of trance sessions once weekly for six weeks on the subject of angels. As you read this book, you'll see how meticulously she has researched from "her side"—the Other Side—and how she's shared her knowledge with us. She addresses each phylum of angels (we now know that there are ten, not just the eight I wrote about in *Life on the Other Side*), and she describes what they look like, whom to call upon, and the specific duties they perform.

At first, these trances were exclusively for the ministers of Novus Spiritus, who said that when Francine imparted her knowledge of angels, they felt the room change, as if they were sitting in the presence of the hosts of heaven. Later, we all agreed that the timing was perfect to include this wonderful information here. No matter what your current beliefs about angels may be, I encourage you to be open-minded as you read this material. Notice the psychic chill of truth I described earlier, and see what, if anything, resonates with you. As always, my slogan is this: *Take with you what you want, and leave the rest.*

A Few Facts and Figures

In one of our first trance sessions, Francine told us that there are trillions of angels. She's never tried to count them, nor has she tried to look up their number in the Hall of Records, the beautiful building on the Other Side that houses every historical work ever written and the detailed chart of every person who's ever lived on Earth. However, she once saw what we might call a readout that listed trillions of angels who populate this planet alone. When you add that to the inconceivable number of angels who populate other planets, they far outnumber anyone of human flesh. At any given time, any living human being could call on tens of thousands of angels, without ever depleting the supply. And that's a lot, considering that there are more than six billion people living on this planet right now.

Angels can interact on both a spiritual and physical level with great power and force. Their strength is legendary, and their ability to take form is also apparent. Their primary purpose is to help us fulfill our written charts as well as their God-given assignment, such as protectorate, messenger, healer, and so on.

One of the most frequently asked questions I hear is typified in this letter from C. She writes:

"Do angels ever take human form for pleasure; that is, without being needed or to aid in a situation? I believe I encountered one once, walking past me in a supermarket. As this older black woman smiled at my baby, it filled me with an indescribable feeling of light, and when I looked back at this woman, who hadn't been moving very quickly down the aisle, she was nowhere in sight. Try as I might, I couldn't find her in the store."

Of course angels take human form for pleasure, and C.'s letter bears up that fact. I sometimes think that they do it to make it easier for us to accept them, rather than appearing in their real form.

I'm often asked whether angels have names. Yes, some religions have given them names such as Michael, Raphael, and Ariel, but angels don't have individual names as our spirit guides do. I'm sure they don't mind what we call them, though . . . as long as we call them. Many times, to make us feel more comfortable, they allow us to call them any name we like. Francine, for instance, has a tendency to call them all Michael. She says it's just easier, but adds that it can also be advantageous to call on the particular group or phylum that can answer your specific need (we'll cover each of these in detail in upcoming chapters).

Believing that we can call on the angels seems to pierce the veil and make them more accessible. Francine says that belief, as our Lord said, can move mountains, but it's also like a hand that reaches through and helps pull the angel closer. If we don't believe, are the angels still there? Of course they are, but our acceptance seems to make it easier for them to come in.

Angels are dispatched by the Council, the governing body of entities on the Other Side. These master teachers are very advanced in their knowledge and spirituality. They help review our charts and, if needed, can insert angels into our charts to help us during a particularly difficult time. As you'll see, nothing in life ever happens by chance. Our charts have been mapped out by not only us, but by this group of highly evolved spirits—as well as our guides, our loved ones, and, last but not least, our angels, who fill in the gaps and help things happen. I like to think of them as the Super Glue of our lives.

Spirit guides and some phyla of angels have been known to petition the Council on our behalf about facets of our charts. Francine, for example, can't change my charted course, but she can consult with the Council on how to help me. Don't think I haven't also petitioned the Council to help me understand a confusing or difficult situation in life. Does it help? Yes, it all helps. The more knowledge we have, the greater our understanding of what we're going through.

I'm often asked how angels were created. Francine has

explained that, from the beginning, we all existed in the mind of God. In fact, she says that the word *beginning* is somewhat erroneous, because there really wasn't a beginning. Since the idea of all of us being created simultaneously is too difficult for most people to understand, she described it in this way:

> "It's not erroneous to say that if we did all exist in the mind of God singularly, there was a delineation of the sparks of the Divine Sparkler. So, for the sake of finite minds (and this is certainly not to discredit anyone's mind), angels were the first creations. If you want to say that we were simultaneously created, you could say that, but let's say the first sparks out were the angels. This was the first beginning of the love. It was almost like a magnificent love affair with God."

When He created angels, God wanted the purest of the pure. This is certainly not to discredit human beings such as ourselves, but angels have no other purpose. Now, some have different careers, jobs, or delineations of what they do, but they're all made out of pure love. Unlike human beings and spirit guides, who have their own individual personalities, characters, likes, and dislikes, angels are nothing but pure love, pure protection, pure knowledge, and pure forgiveness. Angels have no imperfections. They have no other agenda but to help, protect, and love.

They're probably the closest creations to God that we can comprehend.

You may wonder whether angels have thoughts, then. Yes, angels have intelligence, and they have emotion, but it's in the purest form. In other words, angels are not humanized. They don't get mad, despondent, or moody, and there's no such thing as an avenging angel. Since they haven't led lives, they have no cell memories to carry over, no "emotional baggage" or even lessons to be learned. Spirit guides, however, even though they live on the Other Side in a perfect environment of loving, positive energy— what we call heaven—have to become humanized to the point that they can get emotional. If they didn't, they couldn't be effective as guides. In fact, Francine says that's why most spirits don't like to be guides: They have one foot in bliss and the other one in the emotional dimension of Earth. But if it were any other way, they wouldn't be able to answer our questions or relate to our emotions. As Francine has said many times, they would simply say, "Who cares? You'll be over here soon."

What Do Angels Look Like?

Like Francine, Raheim has been my guide my entire life, but since he's a secondary guide, I wasn't aware of him until about 30 years ago. I don't hear him like I do Francine. If he has something to say, he tells her to tell me.

The only time he has a voice is during trance, when he comes in through me and provides information about a particular subject.

In his last incarnation on Earth, Raheim was a Sikh, and apparently a teacher of great renown in imparting knowledge within his faith. Of course, now he's a Gnostic, but let's face it . . . on the Other Side, all religions blend into one because we all have greater knowledge there. Religion down here is a matter of personal preference, whatever road you choose to travel. If you feel that your path of choice is right, then it's right for you.

Raheim tells us that angels represent all the races in creation. There are angels with brown skins, black, red, yellow, and white. Many times they show particular racial characteristics in their eyes, noses, lips, hair, and other facial or bodily features, but there is no prejudice or racial barriers on the Other Side. Angels of all races attend to human beings of all colors and ethnic backgrounds. The faces of angels are not all the same, just as the faces of human beings are not, but their body stature remains the same depending upon their phylum.

Angels are pure, androgynous beings—beautiful, tall, and emanating light. Sometimes the only way you can discern a particular phylum is by their wings, which have either a particular tint in them or a particular color emanating from the tips (we'll discuss the colors further as we explore each individual phylum). This color is also duplicated on the outer fringes of their auras, which are always quite brilliant and which most artists depict as halos.

Jennifer from Indiana writes:

"I've sometimes felt the presence of what I thought were angels in very powerful dreams that I've had. In the dreams, the angels are usually black (dark skinned), and in the last two (especially the one right after my younger brother died), three tall black women in purple were comforting me. My family isn't black, but my older sister also mentioned something about black angels, and my mother said she heard that they were usually very tall. I don't remember my angels having wings, and in one dream the black angel took my hand (it gave me such peace) and said (in my mind) that his name was William. Do these seem like other descriptions of angels?"

Jennifer's letter not only tells a lovely story, but it confirms Raheim's description of angels as beautiful beings who know no racial barriers. Like us, they come in all races, sizes, and forms.

Raheim also describes angels as being basically androgynous in nature, as they have no need for reproductive organs. Elaborating on this topic, Francine tells us that on the Other Side, every spirit has physical characteristics and a sexual gender, as well as "merging ability," the ability of the body and/or spirit to unite with another entity. There's a certain amount of sexuality in the merging process, which is very much like an orgasm of the mind and/or body. Angels, however, do not have this ability. Although some are feminine looking and some are masculine looking, they have no genitalia. They are totally perfect, androgynous beings. They don't have soul mates, they don't live in abodes, and they can't perpetuate their own reality as other entities can on the Other Side.

Oh, Those Beautiful Wings!

So many of us think that we may absolutely know something . . . until we get hit by a proverbial two-by-four filled with some additional information or truth. The following stories show that I'm no exception to this phenomenon.

When I was about 22 years old and newly married to my first husband, I was sitting in my car outside the building where I taught school. It was raining very hard, and I sat there with my head on the steering wheel, thinking that I didn't want to go home. I felt so alone. All of a sudden, there was a knock on the window, and I looked up to see a beautiful man standing there. He had the bluest eyes, steel-gray hair, and a beard. I rolled down the window (something you would never do now), and this man said, "I know you feel alone, but you haven't perfected enough yet to be alone." I stared at him, trying to figure out what he could have meant. I shifted my eyes for a moment, and he was gone. I was shaken by the experience, because I realized I hadn't really heard his words audibly, but more in my mind.

I started the car, and as I began driving home, Francine said, "Well, Sylvia, you just saw an angel."

At the time, I replied, "An angel! No wings, no color."

She said, "Yes, they come as messengers in human form."

From that point on, as some people can attest from attending my early lectures and reading my previous books, I firmly believed that angels didn't have wings. But all that changed in an instant four years ago when I was staying overnight at my son Chris's house.

I'd gotten up in the middle of the night to go from my room across the long entry hall with its high, vaulted ceiling to get a drink of water in the bathroom. Much to my amazement, there in the foyer was a huge—and I mean gigantic—being, the likes of which I'd never experienced. Not only was the height of this being awesome, but it had magnificent, gorgeously colored wings folded carefully into place. As I stood there staring at this beautiful creation for a good two minutes, the angel remained perfectly still as if it were guarding the house. He (and I say "he," even though I know angels are androgynous) seemed more male than female. His face shone like a luminescent light.

I smiled, not really knowing what else to do. As best as I can convey here, the angel smiled softly and with such love, and then this gorgeous entity was gone, or at least gone from my sight, but I still felt the power of its presence around me. This may surprise some of you, but I don't go around being visual all the time. Regardless of my ability, I'm very rooted in reality. Do I see ghosts? Yes, but this was different. It was truly in 3-D, living, solid color . . . and it had wings! I've since learned that an angel's wings are not only real, but on a deeper level they symbolize our freedom. We feel content knowing that these beautiful entities can reach us in the blink of an eye or, as I believe, are with us constantly to wrap their wings of protection around us.

Angel-to-Person Communication

The preceding stories confirm another interesting fact about angels: They rarely speak orally. Francine says that angels can communicate in many ways, but they almost always choose to do so telepathically. A few times, as you'll read in subsequent chapters, people will report that they thought an angel was speaking, just as I did in the encounter in my car. However, looking back, I now know that it was a telepathic communication that was so real that, at the time, I was sure it was actual speech. Only rarely will angels use a voice. In fact, if you think you've heard the voice of an angel, it was probably your spirit guide speaking while the angel was present.

Anne's story is one such example. She writes:

"One memory I have is when I was 30 years of age. I'd been doing genealogical research in a cemetery in a nearby town, and I was headed home. I pulled to a stop at an intersection and did the customary 'look left, look right, look left' before starting to pull out onto the highway. I saw absolutely nothing and I heard absolutely nothing until, as I started to pull out into the road, I heard *'Stop!'* I was so taken by surprise, and so frightened, that I stomped on the brakes just in time to watch a fully loaded, *huge* truck approach from my left and speed by. The truck was definitely surpassing the speed limit; had I pulled into the intersection, it would have hit me broadside, and I surely would have died.

"I sat at the intersection with my heart pounding and my palms sweating. I looked all around me and nobody—*nobody*—was around. No people, nothing. It was a Sunday afternoon, and I can only describe the town as vacant—except for me and that truck. I shakily looked in the backseat. Nothing. I again scanned all around me. Nothing. I then heard a soft, 'You are protected.' Panicking, I looked in the backseat and saw . . . nothing. I went home, and have never told anybody about it until now."

Anne's story provides a great description of angels and guides working in tandem. Angels are often the first to sense danger; they alert our guides, who use their voices to warn us. I've questioned hundreds of people who have had angel sightings, and many times they recall hearing the angels at first. However, when questioned further and in more detail, nearly everyone who's had this experience agrees that the communication was clear in their mind, not their ears.

Not to change the subject, but it bears mentioning here that the same thing happens more often than not with the appearance of loved ones who have passed over: No speech is heard, but a loudly spoken message is conveyed. Why is this so? Well, it seems reasonable to me that thoughts are much less apt to be muddled than spoken words. How many times have you experienced the frustration of being at a loss for words and wishing you could somehow make the other person just feel or hear what was in your mind? Spirits and angels can do just that. Angels can also immediately understand when we're in need. Their vibrational level and makeup of pure, protective loving and healing allows them to comprehend our problems or needs without our having to communicate in words.

Raheim describes an angel's telepathic ability as highly developed and very persuasive. He says that many times guides have been known to recruit a couple of angels to relay a thought to us because their telepathic power, combined with the spirit guide's, can get the thought across more effectively.

Francine says that every time we talk to angels, a fibrous silver thread begins to wind between us and them. It looks cobwebby, but it's not. It's actually quite thick and strong, forming a tentacled webbing, and it appears to contain jewels. When we communicate with the angels, our silvery strands connect with theirs. Usually they hook right into our chakras, which yoga philosophy describes as our body's physical or spiritual energy points. I know that sounds like a painful analogy, but it doesn't hurt. It's simply a painless and miraculous energy connection.

Some people have actually gotten ectoplasm from contact with an angel, as I once did when I was investigating a haunting. I was dealing with a cranky spirit named Judge. He was very unpleasant to me, so an angel stood in front of me to protect my heart chakra. The angel smooshed up against me and accidentally smeared me with its ectoplasm. It was sort of silvery and filmy, according to my assistant, Michael, and several other witnesses who saw it appear.

When I go to bed at night and have a particular problem I'm trying to solve, I always ask God to help me first, then the Christ consciousness, the Holy Spirit, Francine, and the angels. Many times when I've awakened, I've received the answer, and many times my spirit guide has said the answer came from the angels, either telepathically or through infused knowledge (implanted in my mind). While a spirit guide's "voice" can often be more audible than an angel's, never underestimate the power and truth of what angels can impart.

Pure, Unconditional Love

Raheim talks about one last thing that every angel offers, no matter which phylum we consider: unconditional love. No entity, other than God, can ever provide us with the unhesitating magnitude of unconditional love that an angel can. Even spirit guides, who are certainly made out of love and have perfected as much as they can, have limiting conditions. As I said earlier, spirit guides are humanized, and it's this humanity that allows them to become emotional about the entities they watch over. Francine and Raheim become emotional over what they perceive to be injustices to me and my family, just as all guides relate to the injustices that we humans go through. For instance, if we contracted a terrible disease, our guides would be upset and empathetic. Even if we had something minor, like a backache, our guides would be concerned. Angels, however, stand seemingly emotionless and offer a pure, unmitigated, and constant flow of love.

I don't want to give you the idea that angels are mindless. It's just that they haven't had to live a life, so they have no individuality, and they're pure innocence. You won't see an angel stomping around upset or emitting human emotions. Angels are not argumentative and they don't have their own agendas. You won't see an angel going to Council, except in rare instances, and only with a spirit guide who needs to petition for something. For instance, if my guide was having problems with my chart or couldn't get me to listen, she could ask the appropriate angels to accompany her to the Council and help her plead her case.

Angels also don't have much of a sense of humor. In fact, they have none, but they have great joy and a wonderful ability to laugh. You might think, *Well, if they laugh, then they must have a sense of humor,* but their laughter seems to come from a pure joy of the sense of being, not from having a sense of humor. This quality is enviable.

Along with their joy, angels have a static intelligence. I would never say that one angel is smarter than another because they all seem to have the same level of intelligence. One phylum may be higher than another in terms of its power, but not its intelligence. In other words, the Thrones or Principalities may be considered higher phyla than the Angels or the Archangels, but they aren't more intelligent; they simply know their job and do it. Here again, you might ask, "Do the Thrones or Principalities have more love than the Angels or Archangels?" No, they've all reached the same magnificent level of infinite, unconditional love.

Angels are the only creation that can transcend both the Earthly side and the Other Side. They aid, quiet, guide, and help entities on the Other Side just as much as they help us, and in much the same way.

Angels: Fact and Fiction

Before we go any further, let's clear up a few myths about angels. Since we've spent so much time talking about what angels *are,* it's equally important to go over what they *are not.*

First of all, contrary to popular belief, there are no dark angels. Some religious texts warn us to be careful of "evil angels." Others say that Satan is a fallen angel. Not only is there no devil, but Raheim says, "I have never seen a dark angel, ever. There are no evil angels, and there are no dark or fallen angels. The word *angel* itself defies darkness; it's almost like the antithesis of the word *evil.* Angels fight and dispose of evil. They are not in any way evil themselves, just an outpouring of unconditional love."

Another myth about angels is that they come to us singularly. Angels will come to us one at a time, as some of the angel stories included in this book will demonstrate, but it's somewhat of a rare occurrence. Most of the time when angels help us, they're in groups, usually of ten or more—sometimes even in the *thousands* at the scene of great catastrophes. Whether it's a matter of the Virtues going over our charts, the Angels protecting us, or the Archangels and Powers healing us—whatever the purpose—more often than not a group of angels attends us.

When it's written that a band of angels was present, it means exactly that. I find it a little inaccurate to say that only one angel such as Gabriel addressed Mary and told her she was carrying the Christ child. No, Mary was visited by *many* angels, as were all messiah- or messenger-bearing females, from the mother of Islam's founder, Muhammad, to the mother of the Baha'i faith's founder, Bahaullah. Examples of this can be traced all through antiquity in the ancient writings. There's always the heralding of the messenger; there's always a band of angels. Whether it was the shepherds who heard and saw the bands of angels rejoicing at Christ's birth, or those who celebrated the birth of Buddha, throngs of angels have always been present. As the Bible says, their minions will be with us.

The ongoing confusion and myths about angels will probably continue until the end of time, since they seem to have been with us from the beginning, but I hope I've done my part to clear up some of the most common misperceptions.

The Ten Phyla of Angels

As I mentioned earlier, there are ten different phyla or levels of angels.* In the chapters that follow, we'll explore each phylum in detail. For now, the following chart presents an overview of each phylum and its totem, element, representative stone, wing color, purpose, and function.

*Please note that certain words such as "Angels" are capitalized when their phylum is referred to, but not when discussed generally.

Angel Chart

Type of Angel	Totem	Element	Stone	Wings	Purpose	Function
Angels	*Seagull*	*Sun*	*Pearl*	*White with silver tips*	*Protectors*	*Fears and phobias*
Archangels	*Wolf*	*Rain*	*Aquamarine*	*White with blue tips*	*Messengers (they carry the green scepter of healing)*	*Hope*
Cherubim	*Canary*	*Music*	*Quartz*	*White with rose tips*	*Joyous singers*	*Insomnia*
Seraphim	*Canary*	*Music*	*Quartz*	*White with rose tips*	*Joyous singers*	*Remembering dreams*
Powers	*Falcon*	*Moon*	*Emerald*	*White with greenish-white tips*	*Healers*	*Peace*

Type of Angel	Totem	Element	Stone	Wings	Purpose	Function
Carrions	Raven	Wind	Opal	White with an orange tint	Carriers of the dark entities	Fate
Virtues	Dove	Water	Silver	Silver with pale blue tips	Helpers (they help with our charts)	Morals
Dominions	Cougar	Earth	Bloodstone	White with a maroon tint	Overseers of good; recorders of deeds	Strength
Thrones	Elephant	Air	Gold	Purplish white	Azna's (Mother God's) army	Fertility (emotion)
Principalities	Lion	Fire	Sapphire	Gold	Om's (Father God's) army	Justice (intellect)

Angels and Their Totems

The word *totem,* or *anima,* means a living thing that brings about some luck or message. The term comes from American Indian shamans, and literally refers to a person's representative animal. Each of us has a totem, and many times we take on our totem's characteristics. My totem, for example, is the elephant, and like an elephant, I am family conscious, I never forget, and so on. Sometimes groups share a common totem. In the American Indian culture, for example, each tribe has its own totem, an animal that sometimes helps or protects the members of that tribe.

Similarly, each phylum of angels has its own totem, and they're listed in the preceding chart. The angel's totem is its symbol, an animal the angel is sympathetic to and relegated to by way of its phylum. For example, Angels (the first phylum) use the seagull as their way of occasionally showing up. This doesn't mean that Angels appear as seagulls, but that seagulls are their particular animal, specific to Angels. The Archangel's totem is the wolf: swift, enduring, and ferocious when it has to be. The canary, simplistic and beautiful, loves to sing, just like the Cherubim and Seraphim it represents.

All angels can appear to you briefly in the form of their particular anima or totem, but they generally don't do so. Instead, they're more likely to manipulate the energy of your totem or other animals (such as a bear, eagle, hawk, or lion) to appear and speak to you if needed. Raheim says that angels can manipulate animals because they have great power over the dominions of the earth.

In many native cultures, people tell stories of totems that came and spoke to them. With the aid of the angels around them, an animal warned them or protected them from harm. When that happens, it means one of two things: The animal was either the person's own totem, or it was an animal manipulated by an angel. Do not confuse your own totem with that of an angel. An angel may manipulate your totem to speak, but angels rarely take the form of their totems.

Elements and Stones

The element that symbolizes each phylum of angels represents that substance by which the phylum is identified. For example, rain is the element of Archangels. To most people, rain can be dreary or depressing, but stop and think about what rain does. It cleanses, washes, takes care of ulcerations, and purifies, just like the healing of an Archangel. As an aside, no one I know loves rain more than I do, and I have ever since I was a child, although I'm not really sure why.

Each phylum of angels has a corresponding jewel or stone that not only symbolizes what that phylum resonates to but also takes on the power of that phylum. For example, Cherubim and Seraphim have quartz as their stone. These stones can be seen in meditation or, if we're lucky, when we communicate with our angels.

Whom Should You Call?

Each phylum has a particular purpose and can help with emotional functions or problems that show up. Knowing which angel to call on when we need a particular type of help—whether it's a messenger, a protectorate, or a healer—makes it easier to get the job done and helps us feel better. It's not that they don't all come when we call, but do we really need a painter to show up when we want to fix a broken door?

The functions, as listed, are areas of expertise for each phylum, but not necessarily as we humans might interpret. God made the angels, and His idea of a function might be completely different from ours. I would be hesitant to try and give His interpretation, but I do feel that we can pray to a specific phylum for assistance in their function area to perhaps get some help. For instance, in times of stress, we can call upon the Powers for healing (their purpose) as well as peace of mind (their function). Remember, though, that while every phylum of angels has a particular expertise, all angels interact with each other in carrying out their intended function, which is to help and protect all of God's creations.

Does this mean that we have to wear a certain stone or

color, or adopt a particular totem to call upon a certain angel? No, not at all. The information presented in this chapter is just presented for information and knowledge. The more knowledge we have, the more the angels know that we're reaching across the dimensions to bring them closer, and our own faith and belief will help them get through. We can relax, enjoy, and use this new information to call upon the right phylum to help us accomplish even more.

So, how do we call upon our angels when we need them? At the end of each chapter, I've included a meditation like the one below. I recommend recording them onto a tape recorder so you can listen to the instructions as you do the meditation.

MEDITATION FOR CONTACTING YOUR ANGEL

Sit or lie in a comfortable, meditative position. Close your eyes. Relax your feet, your ankles, your calves, your knees, your thighs, and your buttocks area. Relax your body up through your trunk, arms, fingers, neck, and head.

Surround yourself with the white light of the Holy Spirit. Take three deep breaths and transport yourself mentally to the seashore. Make it visually as simplistic or ornate as you wish. As you sit by the beach, lean your back against a palm tree, and put your feet in the warm sand. Feel the waves warm against your feet as the water ebbs and flows. Feel the sun on your face, the wind gently blowing through your hair. Take three more deep breaths, and feel all the negativity seeping out of you with each ebb and flow of the tide.

Ask for an entity, an angel, to join you on the beach. Out of the shadows to the right steps a beautiful being. Invite your angel to approach. Leave imagination out of this. Feel it, sense it. Let the love of God from this messenger envelop you.

Stay as long as you wish. Then, with three deep breaths, bring yourself up from your feet to your head, asking that the light of Mother and Father God, the Christ consciousness, and the Holy Spirit stay with you.

II

The Angels

"For it is written, He shall give His angels charge over thee, to keep thee."

— Luke 4:10

IN 1988, I was driving with Amy, a girl who worked with me in my office. We were on our way to spend the night at my son Paul's house, when we stopped to pick up some sodas and snacks. As we were leaving the parking lot of the store, I happened to look over to my right. Suddenly, I saw a white car bearing down on me from the left, coming too fast and too close for me to get out of the way. I prepared for the impact, and Amy screamed. The air got deathly still, as if time had stopped. There was no impact, no crunching metal, just an eerie silence. Then the everyday noises returned. I looked at Amy, whose eyes were as wide as saucers, and said, "We're probably dead."

I remember getting out of the car somehow, and Amy did, also. Still thinking that we must be dead, I fully expected to see our crumpled bodies, a mass of wreckage, and a tunnel leading to the Other Side. Much to my surprise, there wasn't a scratch—but the car was completely turned around. Always the researcher, I said to Amy, "Don't say a word. Get back in the car, and let's independently write down what we experienced."

Incredibly, our stories were absolutely the same. We both felt the silence and the dreamlike quality of the experience. We talked about it endlessly and knew that angels had truly saved us.

Later, Francine said, "How do you like the way angels can move objects?" And so they did. It wasn't the final exit point for either of us, and our angels had been there to keep us from harm.

Lest you think my experience was unique, here's a letter from a woman named Rose describing a similar event:

"In 1991, I was 22 years old and working in a nearby city. To get to work each day, I had to drive over a four-lane steep hill. A cement divider separated the two directions. This particular day it was a bit overcast, and there were many cars on the road. I was speeding as I came over the top of the hill (the only way to get my little car over it). When I was starting on my way down, the cars in front of me slammed on their brakes. As I slammed on mine, I must have hit some water and started to lose control. I remember sliding down the hill sideways, facing the cement divider. I don't know how my car didn't flip over.

"The next thing I remember, my car was about to slam headfirst into the divider. I closed my eyes and said aloud, 'Please help me, God.' The air got still, and time seemed to stop. I opened my eyes and saw the most beautiful angel, with blonde (almost white) hair, clothed in white—larger than a normal person—with huge wings that were glowing in a brilliant white mist.

I blinked, and she was gone. My car was put back on track in the right direction, in the slow lane. I know I couldn't have done it myself. I *know* it was my angel. I had always believed in angels, and that day I got proof."

Rose's story provides another example of angels moving objects, and it verifies the occurrence Amy and I had while driving to my son's house.

Angels: The Primary Protectors

According to Francine, the first phylum to emerge from creation was the one known simply as the Angels. (Although all the different phyla are known as angels, when I refer to Angels with a capital *A,* I mean this first level or phylum.)

Like all the other phyla, Angels are beautiful and come in many sizes, but mostly they appear to be very tall. They radiate the love and glory of the Holy Spirit and, like all angels, are androgynous in appearance, not showing any gender. They appear in a manifestation of pure, brilliant, white light, almost fluorescent in nature, which emanates from their white, silver-tipped wings to reveal the outline of a beautiful being inside. Their symbol is the sun, indicating their brilliance, and their jewel is the pearl, which signifies the white color of purity.

Their representative totem is the seagull, whose white color again symbolizes purity.

With a population of countless trillions, there are far more Angels than any other category, making them the most likely phylum to enter our lives. Angels are the ones who stand guard around us at night. In fact, they're often referred to as "night angels" because they come around us more at that time than in the daytime. No, we don't wander around during the day without angels, but night has always been the time of the spirit. It's not that we have all kinds of evil spirits coming out of the cracks, but they do come out more at night while we're asleep and at our most vulnerable. You know the old adage of angels being at the four corners of the bed? Well, it's not too far-fetched. Angels do come and stand around our beds, watching over us as we sleep.

As Amy, Rose, and I discovered in our automobile experiences, the Angels' primary purpose is protection. They will go to any extremes to protect their charges. The marvelous thing about Angels is that they can transform themselves more than the other phyla can. They can wrap themselves around the radiator of a car to keep it from exploding, and they can wake us up if there's carbon monoxide in the room. Francine once told me about an Angel who wrapped itself around a tire to keep it from going flat.

Nancy in Houston writes:

"About five years ago, my husband and I were coming back from a once-every-ten-years weekend alone in Louisiana. Chuck was dozing in the passenger seat. I was driving and came upon some folks moving a washer and dryer in the back of a pickup truck. The steering wheel was jerked out of my hands, and we were driving into the other lane just as one of the appliances came flying off the back of the truck and would have landed in our windshield. Chuck was awakened by the noise, and I told him that we were just saved by someone. I felt the presence of an angel/superior spirit and knew that *I* had not driven the car at that moment. I can't explain the forceful jerk of the wheel I felt or the cocoon feeling of the spirit around me. I kept repeating for a half hour: 'We were saved, someone saved us.'"

Angels do have great power. They can move objects, jerk steering wheels, lift cars—and they do all these things with molecular disbursement. Even though we're in a denser environment, Angels, with their higher electrical vibration, can, with God's help, move us out of harm's way. This first phylum has tremendous power beyond our wildest dreams.

Angels are also the phylum that protects children. All entities are protected by both God and His angels, but I feel that children have a special affinity for Angels and vice versa because they have so recently come over from the Other Side, or Home. Lloydine from Florida writes:

"In 1965 I was traveling from California to Colorado. It was the first time I had driven an automatic car, in the snow no less. I started to slide and didn't know how to get the car to stop, but all of a sudden it straightened out. But then my mother-in-law hit the steering wheel, and we went down a 15-foot embankment. When we got to the bottom, the car was facing the hill, there were no tracks in the snow, and we didn't turn and bump around. We just came to sit gently on the ground. On the front seat between my mother-in-law and me was my baby, who was only four months old and had no seat belt or anything. Lying in the back was my two-year-old stepson. Neither of the little ones left the seat, and none of us even got a scratch or bump. I truly believe that my angels saved us. I think they sat that car down gently. I know they're here. I can feel them, and they take ever such good care of me."

Again, this is the same type of experience that Amy and I and so many others have had. Can you see why I get a little crazy when people ask, "What do angels do, anyway?" When we look over our lives, we can easily see near misses we've had that turned our lives around, or warnings we felt deep inside, which, because we heeded them, saved our lives. All of these are examples of Angels and their never-ending desire to protect and watch over us.

Communicating with Angels

Each of us has our own individual Angels. Once we call upon them, they're assigned to us right away, and they don't leave our sides during our lifetime. Francine says that she's even seen some people who got so attached to their Angels in this lifetime that, after they crossed over, they just continued walking around on the Other Side with their whole band of Angels.

Anytime we want to send our Angels to aid or protect someone who needs it, we can. All we have to do is ask, and more Angels will come to watch our loved ones. Many of us have four or five angels around us and can easily get more. We only have to ask.

Angels are God's helpers who come to aid us through this world of strife. Although Angels don't speak, they're telepathic. They can hear our voices, and they can read our thoughts—but only if we give them permission. No angel, entity, or spirit guide can get into our minds without our permission. But if we allow our Angels to read our minds, then we can call on them at any time without verbalization.

To communicate with our Angels, we need only speak as though we were communicating with our spirit guides.

In fact, it's easier to communicate with the Angels than with the guides, because Angels are pure love. Unlike spirit guides, who all have agendas (such as keeping us on track, watching out for our charts, going back to the Council to bicker about a certain issue, and so on), Angels have no thought processes in their minds except for us. They're just pure, loving, protecting beings with open communication channels. We don't have to be in a meditative or altered state to communicate with them. We can just talk to them in a manner in which we feel comfortable, whether it be in the form of a prayer or just everyday conversation. I guarantee that they hear us.

When we speak to Angels, our guides hear it, too. Conversely, if we talk to our guides, our Angels also hear. They all work in tandem. There's no secrecy, covertness, or ego structure. One type of entity doesn't take precedence over another in communication. However, sometimes Angels observe things that spirit guides don't. When that happens, Angels will give information to our spirit guides. Francine says that many of my Angels have given her information that she wasn't aware of.

Angels are both watchful and perceptive; they constantly keep their gaze fastened on us. They notice every quirk, every flick of an eyelash, every twitch of a nose. They've been known to tell the guide, "Wait a minute, I see a shift in the shoulder; I see a grimace," and then the guide begins paying attention to something he or she hadn't noticed before.

Why don't more people use Angels as tools of protection? Probably because they're unaware that Angels are so personal. They may not realize that each of us has Angels who are personally ours, just as we each have one or more spirit guides. Angels are tools of protection who stand as sentinel figures, ready to be the mirrors, the walls, and the swords against negativity. When we have something negative in our minds, we can call on the Angels to infuse us with positive thoughts or suggestions. If anyone can take away depression, it's an Angel. Again, unless we ask, we won't receive. The asking is where the power is. Seek and ye shall find; how many times did Our Lord have to say that? Knock and it shall be opened unto you.

Angels can even rearrange cell memory, which is the memory of past illness contained in the cells of our bodies, either from earlier in this present life or from a past life. If we're definite enough about some ailment, like a bad gallbladder, for instance, we can simply ask, "Can you please help me heal my gallbladder or take away the cell memory of having gallbladder problems?" We must be precise, however; saying something like "I don't feel well" isn't specific enough. And remember, this information is never intended to negate medical intervention.

Even an Angel Can Use a Little Help

Angels serve as the protectorates and activators of daily life. They're here to clean up, fix up, or make way for others. But sometimes even the most powerful Angels need a little help. Occasionally they encounter a situation that's not within their realm of expertise, which is protection. When that happens, they call on other phyla to assist.

To explain further how Angels could need assistance, let's suppose that one of their charges comes down with a severe illness. Unlike some of the other phyla, Angels don't read our charts, so the person's spirit guide would have to convey a warning. The guide might say, "My person is headed for a bad situation." The guide would then call on the Archangels or the Powers (angels who are adept at healing) to assist, or ask the Angels to request help from the Archangels and Powers. Or, if necessary, the Angels could ask some of the higher phyla, such as the Thrones and Principalities, to call on the Council for assistance. Angels themselves can't call on the Council, but in situations of dire necessity, they're the ones who call in the cavalry, so to speak.

As I said earlier, Angels can give messages, but they're not as effective at this as the Archangels. Because Angels are around us all the time—in the trenches, as they say—they relay what they've seen to the Archangels, who aren't around as much. The Archangels can then transmit the message. Usually our guides spearhead all of this, but many times the guides might not be aware of something, so the Angel transmits messages for assistance instead.

Angel Sightings

We've all heard stories of Angels appearing in human form, but we don't always recognize them as Angels at the time of their appearance. Sometimes it's only after the fact that we realize we've had an angel experience.

Susan writes:

"This happened in 1957 or 1958. My husband at the time—we're now divorced—was stationed in England. He and I had gone to the movies, and in the middle of the film, he said he was going to get a few beers, but he would be back to pick me up when the movie was over. When it was done, however, he was nowhere to be found. It was 10:30 at night, very dark and foggy, and I stood there until 12:30, waiting. I had no money at all for a cab, and I was about seven miles from home. While I was standing there, scared, this man appeared and said, 'You shouldn't be out here this time of night alone.' He motioned for a cab, asked where I lived, and gave the cab driver some money. When I got in and turned to thank him, he'd disappeared. My husband came home at three o'clock the next morning, very angry that I hadn't waited. If it hadn't been for this man, whom I've always believed was an angel, I would have had to stand there all those hours."

The actor Mickey Rooney told a story about a young man with golden blond hair who appeared to him in a restaurant when he was thinking about committing suicide. The waiter, who was wearing a red coat with brass buttons, just like all the other waiters, told him, "You don't want to do that tonight. You don't want to take your life." Later, when Mickey told the maître d' that he wanted to thank the beautiful young waiter with the blond hair, the maître d' replied that no one working in the restaurant fit that description. Mickey went through the whole group asking everyone if they knew this person, but they all replied that they didn't. Only then did he realize that an angel had appeared to give him a marvelous message.

Most people can recall an experience where a stranger came to them with a message of some kind or where they felt nudged to turn on a certain TV show or radio station and suddenly received an answer to a problem. Angels are much more powerful than we give them credit for. They're probably some of the most underrated and least-thought-of aspects of creation.

Television talk-show host (and my good friend) Montel Williams has not only been an angel to me and many others on this earth, he also had an Angel appear to him when he was in the hospital. He was literally bleeding out through his nose when he saw an Angel in the corner of the room. The Angel said, "Will you please calm down? Stop. Calm down. Will you please calm down?" Montel was so shaken up that he immediately became calm. He said that the Angel gave him a serenity he'd never felt before.

Not only can Angels take different forms, but they can also cause mass change. N. writes:

> "Many years ago when I worked for a law firm, I developed my monthly severe cramps and decided to go home during my lunch hour and lie down. I did so, but couldn't fall asleep because of the pain. I tried to finally get up and could not. I felt as if I was being held down, but I was alone. I couldn't call out. This went on for a few minutes more, and then all of a sudden I was released. I didn't feel frightened, only confused as to what had happened. As I was driving back to work, I passed a terrible multi-car accident on the road where I would have been driving had I been there a few minutes earlier. I immediately thanked whoever had helped me avoid this possible fatal situation."

I know this was truly an Angel intervention. Why? Because I've gotten so many similar stories and because I had a similar experience myself some years back. Yet, why do some people *never* have an Angel vision? I'm sure they do, they just aren't aware of what they're seeing or feeling. A flick out of the corner of your eye may be an Angel. An instant feeling of well-being or love is an Angel. Theologically, it makes perfect sense that an all-loving God would send loved ones to watch over us. Believing brings with it an energy that makes it easier for Angels to enter. Just the mere fact that we *may* believe helps them come in more readily. Pessimism, despair, and even disbelief become negative blocks. Not believing doesn't mean they're not there; belief just makes it easier to affirm their presence. Belief is energy unto itself that leads to the pathway to our souls.

Far-Reaching Protection

At night, I ask the Angels to surround my home, my children, my grandchildren, my loved ones, and all the people of this earth. In the asking, the Angels do come, and as my knowledge has increased, I've noticed that calling on the specific phylum seems to make a huge difference, too.

Psalm 91:10–12 tells us: "There shall no evil come to thee; nor shall the scourge come near thy dwelling. For He hath given His angels charge over thee; to keep thee in all thy ways. In their hands they shall bear thee up; lest thou dash thy foot against a stone." It's interesting to note that in this psalm as well as in other religious writings, from the early Vedas to the Dead Sea Scrolls, Angels protected not only people, but also Earth itself, and all the creatures that inhabit this planet. However, I cannot emphasize enough that no spirit guide or angel should ever take the place of the loving God of creation. I don't want anyone to get lost in angels, saints, or any other entities and forget who the ultimate Big Boss really is. Use them as an addition to your life and as an army of good to fight darkness.

I, like you, have gotten impatient when darkness descends and I feel alone in my desert period . . . and I sometimes feel as if God is on vacation. But I persevere, and I encourage you to do the same, because I know that everything will come to good, especially if we keep our eyes on the target, which is to let no one dissuade us from the universal law that our Lord taught: to do unto others as we would have them do unto us. When we're on this track, we make it easier for the angels to attend us.

Jason writes:

"My mother believed in angels. She collected them for many years. Memorial Day 1999, while vacationing in Mexico with her friends, she was involved in a fatal car accident. My family received her luggage a few days before her memorial service. Inside her bag we found rolls of undeveloped film. We had the film developed and were able to timeline her vacation, and one of the last pictures was of a narrow dirt road and the sky. In the sky, we noticed that one of the clouds was in the perfect shape of an angel. Since this picture was of nothing but the road and sky, we think she noticed the angel, too, and took a picture of it. She was killed shortly afterwards. We pray that the angel was with her in the car and carried her to heaven."

This is typical of so many of the letters I've received: stories of angels in the sky, in front of a car, inside a car. Of course, this angel took Jason's mother directly to heaven, or as we say, to the Other Side, and she felt no pain and died instantly. Not only do our guides come when it's time for us to cross over, but our loved ones and our angels are with us as well.

This next story, even though a little long, validates so many elements of the angel stories I've received. It also validates my own experience that not only do angels come with wings and glorious colors, but they come in human form.

Darlene writes:

"God sent my guardian angel to help me on a Saturday morning in April 1982. My husband had to work that day, so I was home alone with our two young daughters (ages four and eight). I set about doing my Saturday chores, which included gathering all the trash from the house and burning it in the backyard burn barrel. We live out in the country in the Wisconsin prairie. The snow was all melted that April, and the prairie grass was just beginning to dry out in the spring winds.

"Those spring winds decided to take the fire out of the burn barrel and into the prairie grass. By the time I noticed it, the fire had begun to spread (luckily away from the house). I called my neighbors Shirley and Mike to help me. We didn't have the garden hose out yet, so we just grabbed rugs and began to wet them from the outside faucet to beat out the fire. The wind picked up, and we began to quickly lose the battle. I then called the fire department.

"I ran back outside to help, and that's when my angel appeared. At that time, there were dirt bike trails all through the area in the back of our house, so at first it didn't seem strange to see this person appear on a motorcycle. He (I'm guessing it was a male because he had a motorcycle helmet on with a dark sun visor covering his face) got off the motorcycle and began to walk along the fire line and put the fire out. It seemed like an eternity as I watched cedar trees go up in balls of flame before the fire department finally arrived. They got lost, which is another story. We live near Lake Wisconsin, and they went to the wrong side of the lake. But the fire was out by the time they arrived. I ran to tell the firemen not to take any equipment off the truck, and by the time I got back to the fire area, my angel had disappeared as fast as he had appeared. None of us saw him ride off or had a chance to thank him.

"Mike, Shirley, and I just stared at each other in utter amazement. We all knew right then that it was an angel. We were battling feverishly with those wet rugs, and my angel just calmly walked along the fire line until it was out. Usually it was just kids on dirt bikes who rode those trails. None of us had ever seen a person (my angel) dressed like that before, and none of us have seen him since.

"I know in my heart that God sent me an angel that day. Before the movie *Michael,* some people scoffed at my story, because they thought angels only come in glorious white outfits with wings and all, but my angel came to me dressed in a motorcycle helmet with a dark sun visor, black leather jacket, black leather gloves, and heavy boots, and I thank God for him."

The stories sprinkled throughout this book show not only that angels can take form, but also, as Francine says, that they can come in all guises. As the Bible tells us in Hebrews 13:2: "Do not neglect to show hospitality to strangers, for by this some have entertained angels without knowing it."

MEDITATION FOR PROTECTION AND PEACE OF MIND

Sit or lie in a comfortable, meditative position. Close your eyes. Relax your feet, your ankles, your calves, your knees, your thighs, and your buttocks area. Relax your body up through your trunk, arms, fingers, neck, and head.

Relax and take three deep breaths. Surround yourself with your angels. Ask them to fold their wings around you. See yourself in a magnificent temple where rows and rows of angels are singing the glory of God. Feel the love and colored lights emanating from these glorious beings. Feel the love permeating your being and rinsing away all despair, all ignorance, all fear. Feel the light of God shining upon you and releasing you from guilt, regret, and even illness. Stand in this marble temple and feel that you are blessed by heaven. Lie there and relax, and feel the peace.

This is a good meditation to use before going to sleep. It clears your mind, helps you know that you're protected, and also keeps bad dreams away.

III

The Archangels

"All praise be to Allah, Who created the heavens and the earth, Who made the angels Messengers with wings, two, three, or four."

— Koran 35:1

LIKE THE other angels, Archangels, the second phylum on the angel chart, don't have individual names, although Francine likes to call them all "Michael." Their symbol or element is rain, which signifies the cleansing and healing they do. Their jewel is the aquamarine, whose blue color matches the tips of their otherwise white wings and signifies tranquility and the all-encompassing sky. Their totem or anima is the wolf, a symbol of their swiftness and endurance as messengers, which is their stated purpose.

We can call on the Archangels to send messages to other angels or to another person. If you don't believe me, try this little experiment. Ask the Archangels to send a message to your son or daughter, or someone you haven't heard from in a while, and request that they call you. Don't be afraid to ask the Archangels to prove their validity; they have no problem with being tested, and they won't be upset. Unlike spirit guides, who have been known to go to the Council and raise holy hell over something bad in our lives, Archangels don't know the meaning of the word *upset.*

Archangels, like the Angels and all the other phyla, are facilitators. They're the embodiment of God's love, and they're here because God knows that it's important for us to be surrounded by these celestial messengers. We should never say, "Oh, I couldn't call on an Archangel. They're too evolved." We can and should call upon them and let them serve their primary purpose on our behalf.

The following letter from Sandra shows that angels are always with us. When we're privileged to see and hear them, whether in their "angel form" or as messengers in human form who bring us a message of hope or warning, it's a wonderful envelope in time.

Sandra writes:

"In the summer of 1989, I was almost into my third month of pregnancy, as I had just found out that Friday afternoon from a home pregnancy kit. I was ecstatic. Married three years, I was ready. My doctor had taken me off the Pill a couple of weeks earlier because I'd been experiencing what I thought were some bad side effects. When I called the doctor on Monday morning with my news, he told me to come right over, and I did. After a brief exam, I was sent to get an ultrasound. I should have known then that something was up. Back to my OB/GYN I went, who informed me that the pregnancy was tubular and I would require immediate surgery. Right then and there, he phoned the hospital and booked me for the next morning. I asked to speak to the anesthesiologist because my aunt had died just six months before; she was allergic to the anesthesia and died before getting started.

"I went under fast, and in the blackness I saw a light coming to me at great speed. It was so bright, brighter than anything I've ever seen, and then I saw her—an angel so totally perfect. I've never felt so much love as she gazed at me with those lovely eyes. She spoke to me—I don't recall in what language—but I could hear her and she could hear me. She told me not to worry, that everything would be fine. She put her arms up as if to embrace me, but we never touched. I wanted to go with her and selfishly leave everyone behind. I noticed that her wings were taller than her head, and there were lights on them. The skin was like porcelain, and she had beautiful long blonde hair. Describing her doesn't do her any justice. I'll never forget her or her beauty as she came to comfort me. She smiled at me, and the light moved back far away till she was gone.

"Everything went dark again until I awoke that evening. The first thing I said to the nurse was that I'd been visited by an angel; she smiled at me and brought my family in. As I lay home recovering, all I could do was think about her. I told my husband, my mother, and my sister Patty. They didn't believe me then; I think they do now.

"For years after that experience that I keep so close to my heart, I've also had other things occur to me every now and then. As I almost drift off to sleep, I often feel feathers touching my face. I've gotten up many times, turned on the lights to see if something was on me, but nothing. As I fall asleep, I'm caressed, and I feel so loved. Even though I don't see her, I feel her."

Sandra's letter, like so many of the hundreds of letters I've received, includes many of the same tenets that everyone reports: the telepathic communication and the wonderful feelings of safety and security. It's interesting to note how the angel's wings glowed. I'm convinced that this type of glowing is a healing emanation, offering the comfort of God's love.

The Scepter of Healing

As Sandra's letter illustrates, not only do Archangels carry messages, they're also instruments of healing. When summoned, Archangels arrive swiftly. In fact, Francine says that they sometimes come in with a bang! They don't sweep the other angels away, but when an Archangel appears, all the other angels show a deep respect.

Archangels carry what Francine describes as the baton or scepter of healing. An Archangel's baton comes from a gorgeous, emerald-green pond inside the Hall of Wisdom, an orientation center on the Other Side. When someone is in a bad situation and requests their help, the Archangels pick up their beautiful green batons from the almost crystal-like water, and carry them straight to that person. They touch the person with the baton, right in the heart chakra.

The healing baton has a beautiful round crystal ball on each end, and it glistens. It has a gripping handle in the middle with two round and beautiful orbs that turn almost crystal green. When the person is touched in the heart chakra, the whole baton turns dark, absorbing the illness or negativity. It's amazing to see it turn jet black when an Archangel performs a healing. Afterward, the Archangel returns to the pond and dips the scepter into the water, smiling as the baton becomes clear again. Not that Archangels cry, but they're more somber when a baton hasn't done anything. They're always so happy when a healing takes place—not because of pride, but because a mission has gone well.

If the baton doesn't turn dark, that means there's nothing the Archangel can do. The person's chart has overridden his or her request. Now, by no means should we ever get the idea that the darkness comes from some bad humor or spell or anything like that. We should never, ever take that into consideration or even think such a thing. Sometimes a person can't be, or is simply resistant to being, healed, maybe on the subconscious or superconscious level. We certainly shouldn't feel bad if we can't facilitate a healing for someone, because their own will or their chart can at times override our desires.

Archangels and Azna, the Mother God

As tragic as it may sound, the person (or someone working on his or her behalf) must ask for Archangels to intercede. Francine has known of a few Archangels who helped people because Azna, the Mother God, directed them to do so. In those cases, the Archangel knew that God wanted them to be healed, or it was in their chart to be healed, or Azna had interceded for them to be healed, and it was a marvelous healing. But most of the time, the person or someone working on his or her behalf has to ask the Archangels for healing. So, anytime you want to facilitate a healing for someone (for example, all the people who have AIDS), call on the Archangels.

For those who may not have read any of my other books, it bears mentioning here that all religions, including Christianity, have featured female counterparts to the male deities. It's almost ridiculous to believe that God has only a male side, and virtually none of the major religions would agree. I'm sure that God doesn't care what name we give Her, whether it's Azara, Theodora, Sophie, Isis, or some other name. In Catholicism, it was Mary. In Turkey, it was Anatol. In Buddhism, it's the Lady of the Lotus. In our Gnostic church, we call Her Azna, which is the ancient Gnostic name for Mother God. The reason She bears mentioning here is not only for clarification, but because so many of the angels answer to Her call.

Azna carries the symbol of a golden sword, which, you

may have noticed, is the same shape as a cross. Her sword is not a symbol of harm, but rather a sign that She can cut through the darkness and negativity of this world that some call school (or hell, as I choose to call it). When called on to dispel darkness, Azna wields Her sword to part the darkness and leave light and hope. I can only advise you that if you want prayers answered, ask Azna. I have thousands of affidavits attesting to this. People who ask Her or petition Her, as well as calling on Her minions of angels, get their requests answered quickly.

We can also call upon Azna and the Archangels to help us in our everyday lives. I hear so many people expressing the idea that they're afraid to ask for help for themselves. We should never feel that way. If we ask on our own behalf, Azna and her angels will come to our aid.

Archangel Visits

The following letter from Terri tells of two angel visits that certainly could have been from Archangels:

"When our son was four, he became very ill with a respiratory problem, and I was very scared. I had read that mothers' prayers for their children are heard first and loudest. I began to pray, 'Now, I want proof that you're hearing me. Please help my son. We need all the angel help we can get to help him breathe! Please help him!' We then got him ready to go to the hospital, and I forgot about my prayer.

"As we headed for the hospital, our son looked out the car window and said, 'Mom, look at all those angels going to the hospital with us!' I couldn't see them, so he told me they were 'up by the clouds and one is so pretty.' As we pulled into the hospital parking lot, I asked if they were still with us. He said in an irritated voice as he looked up to the clouds, 'Yes, Mom. I told you they're coming to the hospital with us!' His fever broke, and his breathing became normal in the car on the way to the hospital. They sent him home on antibiotics. I guess I got my proof!

"The birth of our fourth son was a miracle, too. After reading one of Sylvia's books, I truly feel that this was an exit point for both of us. The doctor asked if I realized that God had held my hand all the way to the hospital. Anyway, at the hospital and for about a week after coming home, I could see a shadow always around our son. I kept asking people if they could see it, and everyone thought it was too much pain medication. That's when I started to investigate angels, and feel I saw his angel helping him to get better faster than the doctors could believe, with no residual effects."

Emotional Healing

Archangels can be called upon to heal specific areas. If we're terribly depressed, we can ask for the Archangel to come and put the baton on our heads. If we're broken-hearted, we can ask for the baton to be put at our hearts. We can also ask the Archangels to put their batons on our children for any illnesses they may have. Illness is not always physiological, and we shouldn't hesitate to call upon the Archangels for any mental or emotional healing we might need.

Sierra from British Columbia writes:

"I'd like to share an account of angels as told to me by my father. On September 11, 2001, my father and his friend Harvey went together to get Harvey's RV repaired. While they were waiting, my dad suggested going outside, since it was a nice day. Once they were outside, my dad looked up at the sky and saw the most brilliant angel. At first he thought it was a cloud, but this was a cloud that wasn't changing shape, and it had the most unbelievable light coming off of it. It was a light my dad had never seen before on Earth.

"Still thinking that he was seeing things, he pointed it out to his friend, who was also awestruck. The angel remained in the sky for several minutes. This event occurred at the time the

Twin Towers and the Pentagon had been hit. When my dad told me, he almost thought that no one would believe him. He said to me that no one could ever convince him that there was not a God. This stands out in my mind as a most powerful message about the power and comfort angels provide as they link us to the majesty of God's love."

This is so true, and a wonderful story of inspiration. At the time of 9/11, there were many stories of people seeing angels, which of course shows that God sent his legions of blessed angels to escort those dearest of souls to the Other Side and to bring the rest of us a message of hope.

Astral Travel

The Archangels can heal, and they can carry messages, and they can do one more thing as well. They can take us out of our bodies and take us away on an astral trip. To go on an astral trip, or what some people call an out-of-body experience, we can call on the Archangels to help us, because these messengers can be the ones who come forward and whisk us right up. Or, if astral travel isn't your thing, just remember to call on the Archangels anytime you want to send a message, ask for healing, or need a little hope.

MEDITATION FOR HEALING
(from the Archangels)

Sit upright, back straight, head balanced easily on your shoulders. Close your eyes. Relax your feet, your ankles, your calves, your knees, your thighs, and your buttocks area. Relax your body up through your trunk, arms, fingers, neck, and head.

Take three deep breaths and ask that the white light of the Holy Spirit surround you, and that Mother and Father God's love enter into every cell in your being. Feel the Christ consciousness in front of you. Now begin to visualize the angels, tall and stately, with their wings outstretched. See them as they come closer and form rings around you, standing as sentinel figures of light. They give off a pearlescent glow. They are there for your protection.

In the outside ring, moving closer to you, are the Archangels, glowing with a blue iridescent color. Immediately, you see a type of baton in their hands, crystal-like with large round orbs at each end. The Archangels approach you lovingly. If you feel pain or distress, ask them to heal you with their scepters. If not, let them just run their scepters over you to absorb any illness, pain, or negativity. Sit there quietly, allowing the grace and the breath of this moment to seep into your soul.

Begin to bring yourself up, breathing deeply.

*Before you come all the way up to consciousness, ask
the angels to stay or come whenever you need them.
Now bring yourself all the way up. One . . . two . . .
three . . . four. . . . Come up and out, feeling marvelous.*

You can do this meditation as many times as you wish.
I think it's particularly effective at night.

IV

The Cherubim and Seraphim

"And suddenly there was with the angel a multitude of the heavenly army, praising God, and saying: Glory to God in the highest; and on earth peace to men of good will."

— Luke 2:13–14

LET'S TAKE a peek at two of the most joyous phyla of angels, the Cherubim and Seraphim, shown at levels three and four on the angel chart. Their element is music, and although some people might not think of music as an element of nature, we need to remember that nature makes its own music. The anima or totem for both these phyla is the canary, which relates directly to their main purpose of being God's heavenly choir. Their stone, quartz, signifies all the different refractions of the tones and vibrations in their music.

Cherubim are slightly larger in stature than Seraphim, but both have huge, broad, snowy white wings with rose-colored tips. Their wings stand high above their heads and fold down closer to their bodies than the wings of Archangels. Did you know that an angel's wing tips actually glow? They're luminescent, and they appear to be lit from somewhere inside. The closest analogy I can give you is the phosphorescence of deep-sea animals. The colors of an angel's wings are intended not only for recognition, but also as a representation of their powers or function; the glowing colors are similar to the wearing of a badge. In the case of Cherubim and Seraphim, their rose-colored wing tips represent love.

The only other distinction between the two phyla is

that Cherubim have a singing ability, while Seraphim have a vibrational and tonal ability. The melding of the two in song is not only inspirational, but produces music that is out of this world in its beauty, harmony, and sound.

God's Heavenly Choir

Cherubim and Seraphim were created to sing—and oh, what singing! On the Other Side, their primary purpose is to stand in the spectacular structure known as the Hall of Voices and sing, filling the atmosphere every day with the joy and happiness of their music. As the various entities on the Other Side go about their daily activities, such as research, teaching, orientation, animal husbandry, or whatever part of the schematic they've chosen, they hear the Cherubim and Seraphim singing. Francine says that it's so common that, while the entities on the Other Side don't exactly take it for granted, they're always aware of songs filling the air. She calls it "choir practicing." You might wonder why angels would need to practice, since they're such elevated beings, but the Cherubim and Seraphim are always composing and learning new music.

Throughout time, the Cherubim and Seraphim have been known as the choirs of the hosts of heaven. When Jesus Christ was born and at many other great celebrations or feast days, the hosts of heaven were present, singing the hallelujahs. Francine says that one of the things everyone on the Other Side looks forward to with great expectation is hearing the new songs these joyous singers come up with for celebrations.

On the Other Side, their celebrations often coincide with ours, although there are different ones, too. Entities on the Other Side call these the "high celebratory days," or the "high holy days," a term they've "borrowed" from us. Well, maybe *borrowed* isn't exactly the right word. Even though Aramaic is the universal language, spoken telepathically on the Other Side, as entities have incarnated into lives here on Earth and then returned Home again, the language has become somewhat "polluted" with the adoption of some of our slang words and derivatives.

You might wonder what kind of music these heavenly composers produce. On the celebratory days, Francine says that the marvelous music permeates into her very cells. She describes it as similar to Claude Debussy's beautiful song "Clair de Lune," and explains that the music contains more melody than the "heavier" compositions by Mozart or Bach. Some of the pieces are anthem-like creations that no one could sing. They don't always have words, and they're not operatic. They're more like vibratory tones that penetrate deep into the soul. The Cherubim and Seraphim seem to know every tone, sounds that no human being has ever heard. They're vibratory in nature, similar to a tuning fork but not that high-pitched, and they emit a force that can actually be felt.

After the particular trance session in which Francine

described the music of the Cherubim and Seraphim, I came out of trance to find Mary Simonds, one of my precious ministers, crying. I became immediately concerned and asked, "Mary, did Francine say something to upset you?"

"No," she answered. "Many years ago something happened to me that I've never told anyone. It was a time when I was so despondent and felt my life was coming apart. I was coming home and looked up in the sky, and there was a host of angels singing. I'm not sure of the words, I just knew it was a sound that I've never experienced before or since. It filled my soul so fully that I stopped crying and felt full of peace, comfort, and love."

Mary, I can tell you, is never given to fantasy, but there it was—instant validation. By the way, it bears mentioning that I'm never aware of what goes on when I'm in trance. I had to listen to the tape of the trance session so I could hear and understand the full information that Francine had given. As a deep trance medium, a state that can be truly disconcerting at times, I often feel when I go into trance that everyone else gets to receive the knowledge or have the fun . . . while I have to "go away."

Angelic Voices Here on Earth

The experience Mary Simonds described was highly unusual. Unlike the other angels we've explored so far, Cherubim and Seraphim are rarely seen or heard on this planet. Out of the hundreds and hundreds of letters I've received about angel sightings, I'd say that no more than ten or so have described the music produced by the Cherubim and Seraphim. For the most part, these heavenly singers don't appear to us as often as other angels do. There is, however, a well-documented case concerning three children who went out in a field and heard joyous music.

Another well-documented case took place in England around April 1876. Twenty people were having a picnic when, all of a sudden, one of the women looked up. There in front of her were angels that seemed to be floating about three feet off the ground, singing their hearts out. Wondering what made their friend so excited, the other 19 witnesses also turned to look, and they saw the same thing she did.

Now, two things happened here. First, because the atmosphere in England is heavy with condensation, which causes the frequent dense fogs we hear so much about, it can transmit electrical force. Second, the location of the picnic happened to be in the exact location in which the Hall of Voices stands on the Other Side. In other words, the electrical force acted as a conductor, carrying the music from the Hall of Voices to the picnic in England.

If this seems a little confusing, let me elaborate. As I explained in *Life on the Other Side,* the topography of the Other Side corresponds exactly to the topography here on Earth. Our continents, mountains, rivers, lakes, oceans, and forests all exist in their original perfection—along with Earth's two lost continents, Atlantis and Lemuria. The resulting nine continents on the Other Side are each divided into quadrants, and the Hall of Voices just happens to stand in the location that corresponds with England on our side. So, atmospheric conditions being just right, those 20 picnickers were able to tune in to the angelic singing taking place inside the Hall of Voices.

A similar story was told in a letter I received from a woman who was sitting in her house and thought she heard someone playing "angelic music." She went to her backyard and discovered that the music was permeating her entire household. Although she didn't understand what was happening, it was simply a matter of condensation in the air, a heavy telepathy similar to what had occurred in England more than a century ago, transmitting the music like a telephone receiver.

Healing Powers

The vibrations and tonal qualities of the Cherubim and Seraphim's music are more than just beautiful and inspiring; they can also be used for healing. Although these joyous singers rarely leave the Hall of Voices on the Other Side, it's only because they're not called upon like the other more active phyla. However, Francine says that if we call them, they will come, and she has often witnessed the healing effects of their music.

Angels automatically know which vibrational level a person needs for healing, and the "heavenly choir" sings in that vibration zone and can help immensely with the healing process. The vibration and tones of their music seem to have a healing effect on the electrical makeup of the human body. Francine also notes that when Cherubim and Seraphim sing in the course of the healing process, they spiral up into the air to the point of looking like dots. This fascinating spiraling effect emulates our own DNA, with the music permeating each and every one of our cells.

Cherie from Washington writes:

"About 20 years ago, I experienced something that I'll never, ever forget. I was around 19 or 20 years old, and I remember being very depressed, hopelessly depressed—not over a boyfriend or anything like that, just this deep depression I'd experienced before, even as a baby. It was around 10:15 P.M. or so when I was lying in my bedroom and heard this sound. The best way I can explain it is like chanting, but not a song, and I remember the music. It's something I'd never heard before. It was so eerie, to be honest, that it scared me to death. My dad was crippled, and he slept very lightly, if at all, at night, so I was anticipating him getting up to investigate; which, I might add, he'd done before on numerous occasions when there was something out of the ordinary. This night he didn't, so I just laid there, and it went on for a good 20 minutes, or so it seemed.

"The next morning, we were eating breakfast and I asked him what that sound was last night. He had no idea what I was talking about, and he claimed he was awake. So I investigated it (mind you, during daylight hours). I tromped around in the woods for a while (I just knew it was devil worshipers or a cult thing), and I remember thinking, *How brazen of them, so close to our house in the country. Couldn't they find other places to go?* But as I looked around, no fire pits for their sacrifices, no nothing . . . just woods and brush. That sound was *right* outside my bedroom window, as if they were camped right there!

"So I talked myself into dismissing it, although I couldn't get it out of my head. The next night rolled around. I was reading, still under this never-ending gloomy cloud, and I started to hear this chanting, for lack of a better word. I looked at the clock, and it was at the exact same time as the night before. I was so scared that I got mad, turned out my lamp, and opened the shutters to my bedroom window, thinking I would catch them . . . but nothing—no fire, no light of any kind. I opened the window, and this sound wasn't outside either, it was *all around me!* I climbed back into bed and started to listen, and the most peaceful feeling came over me. I was in tears. There are no words to describe the sound I was hearing—music, but with musical instruments I had never heard before and knew didn't exist here on Earth. So I just tried to absorb all of it. It was absolutely beautiful, and then it quit. I again looked at the clock, and it ended at exactly the same time as the previous night.

"Night number three, I waited, praying to God for it to come, and it did, same time, same place. This time I just totally savored every second of every minute. The most beautiful voices I'd ever heard—not even Charlotte Church could hold a candle to this—no one here could. Sadly, the story ends here. No number four. What was it? Were they angels singing to me? I've never heard them again and have been in that deep despair many times since."

Cherie's letter is definitely a story of the heavenly choir of the Cherubim and Seraphim singing. Their music is like no other, and to hear their sound is indeed a once-in-a-lifetime experience. Although most angelic healing is done by Archangels (with their batons) and Powers (with their wings, which you'll read about in a later chapter), there have been instances when the Cherubim and Seraphim helped them by using vibratory singing. This is especially true in terminal illness cases.

To call upon the Cherubim and Seraphim for help in our own lives, we can use the following meditation.

MEDITATION FOR HEALING AND REJUVENATION

Put yourself in a relaxed position, either sitting or lying down. Close your eyes. Relax your feet, your ankles, your calves, your knees, your thighs, and your buttocks area. Relax your body up through your trunk, arms, fingers, neck, and head.

Surround yourself with a multicolored light this time, reflecting iridescent white, green, blue, and coral. Make these colors swirl around you. Now take yourself to a beautiful Romanesque building, cathedral-like in its appearance and filled with high marble pillars and shimmering lighted candles that dance and sparkle everywhere. At first you may feel very small, but as you proceed down the aisle of this beautiful place, you feel your strength of body, mind, and soul becoming stronger. Right before you reach what looks like a tiered altar, you see these beautiful angels. Their wings are glowing, their faces shine, and they are all looking at you with love, compassion, and understanding.

As you stand there filled with boundless love, you begin to hear music. It is not only outside of you, but resonating on the inside. It is as if every cell is filled with glorious sound. The music is not loud but pulsating, healing, and orgasmic. You feel so full of the love of God and this heavenly choir. Stand there for as long as you want, and let this blessed sound fill your soul. Then slowly back out, carrying with you the song of the angels.

Go to your cathedral as many times as you wish. Each time you'll feel more healed and more rejuvenated.

V

Two New Phyla: The Powers and the Carrions

"So it will be at the end of the age; the angels will come forth and take out the wicked from among the righteous."

— Matthew 13:49

IN *LIFE on the Other Side,* I wrote about eight phyla of angels. Until recently, when Francine presented new information in the series of research trance sessions that preceded this book, I was unaware of two additional phyla: the Powers and the Carrions. In this chapter, we'll explore them both.

The Healing Ability of the Powers

Like Archangels, the fifth phylum of angels, the Powers, have healing as their primary function. Unlike Archangels, though, the Powers don't need a scepter or green-orbed baton to facilitate healing. In fact, the Powers don't use artifacts of any kind; they bring only themselves, using their beautiful wings to form a protective canopy around the person who needs their healing abilities. What the Archangels can't do, the Powers can, as they literally surround the person with their wings.

Powers are large in size, even to the point of being huge. Some are average to medium, but they all have the capability of becoming enormous. The Powers' totem is the falcon, whose swiftness and perseverance emulates the Powers' created purpose. Their element is the moon, again not an *element* in nature, but a *part* of nature, signifying the female or motherly aspect. The Powers' stone is the emerald, which, like the Archangels' baton, radiates the healing color of green. Powers' wing tips are also a greenish white, with what we perceive as a blue electrical flame shooting out. When we call on the Powers, they not only shelter us with their canopy of wings, they give off an electrical or magnetic emanation that goes directly into our bodies and acts as a healing force.

When we unleash the powerful healing ability I've just described, we can use it to ward off or minimize illness. Illness is nothing more than an entrance into the body left unguarded. I don't want to give the impression that I'm going back to the Indian (from India) belief that all negativity results from a bad humor that entered the body, like a demonic possession. Let me explain this in a simpler way.

Every day of our lives, we face, and must live in, a negative environment. We have defenses for fighting this negativity: our immune system, our mind, our energy, our genetics, and our cell memory, which contains the memory of each cell in our bodies throughout our total existence as a created entity. If our defense systems are not utilized and attended to, our immune systems break down and our cell memory kicks in. Our minds may not be aware of what's going on, our energy and outlook may sag, and we start transferring the programming we take in every day. We hear, "Gee, Mabel, you don't look so good today," or "Harry, you look like you need some sleep," and we begin developing an illness.

Illness is a reality of the human body, but if we're going to get a cold or flu, why not have it for 15 minutes rather than 15 days? The immune system is linked directly to cell memory. When we make our cell memory, which is basically sentient, aware that it can fight, we start creating internal armies to dispel illness. When we program our minds to be positive, eat the proper foods, and get enough rest, we complete these internal armies. Then we can bring in our external armies, our angels. They're the precipitators of healing, as well as messengers. Not only will the lower phyla of angels heal us physically, but the higher phyla, the Virtues and Principalities, will heal us mentally as well.

Powerful Stories of Healing and Love

I've received so many letters from people who wrote that when they said prayers and sent an angel to a friend or loved one, the person was either healed or saw the angel or both. Miracles are all around us if we believe. As our Lord says, ask and ye shall receive. This applies in all situations, so we need to remember to send angels to others as well as ourselves.

R. T. writes:

"Recently, a friend of mine was having a difficult time with her asthma. I didn't know this, but had a feeling that something was wrong, so I asked God to send an angel to come around and protect her. The next day when I spoke to her, she said that during the asthma attack, an angel walked in and sat on the bed with her. The angel stayed with her all night long, and in the morning she was better. Now she truly believes in angels and spirit guides."

Marion writes:

"I have seen an angel. It was approximately four inches tall and very brilliant white, but it didn't hurt my eyes to look at it. Its wings were almost as large as its body, and it had on a white gown that ended at its feet. It appeared when I was at the end of my rope, a time when I was almost totally exhausted from helping my sisters care for my mother, who had liver cancer; my dad, who had emphysema; and also two sisters and a brother with Rothmund-Thomson syndrome. With all the trips to the doctors for treatments, and caring for so many at the same time, I became utterly exhausted. Sleep was not easy to come by, since all the day's activities would continually flow through my head.

"One night as I struggled to say my prayers, I looked over to the bedroom door, and in came a little white light. It circled three times over the bed and rested on my sleeping husband's shoulder— just in front of my face. I only had time to identify it as a tiny angel. As I looked at it, I felt a warm, comforting peacefulness and must have fallen asleep instantly. The next thing I remember, it was morning. That was the first night I had slept soundly in months. After that, I didn't see the angel, but its visit remained in my mind and gave me the peace I needed to relax and fall asleep. With much-needed rest, it was possible to carry on. As for my family, I always knew what the outcome would be. I guess what I really wanted was the strength and energy to care for them. God gave that to me, in the form of a tiny angel. I only hope my sisters got an angel, too."

They did; everyone does.

Even though Marion knew what the outcome would be for her loved ones, this was an example of an angel transmitting peace and tranquility to help her get through a painful journey here on Earth. It also validates again that angels can come in all sizes, shapes, colors, and even in human form. Angels don't normally come in a form this small, but they can. They're generally very tall and huge in stature, but they sometimes change their shape or size to fit the situation.

The Carrions

No other group of angels does what the Carrions do. This sixth phylum of angels carries away the dark entities when they die. Dark entities are the ones that separated from God in the beginning of creation. Nobody touches dark entities except the Carrions, who literally grab them and escort them to their own holding place in God's creation. A Carrion's only mission is to stand very far back until a dark entity is ready to pass over at death.

Carrions were created as a protection for other entities, both in our world and on the Other Side. They're the reason dead evil entities don't roam the earth. There are disruptive entities, and entities who don't know that they're dead, but the Carrions don't let the dark entities stay around. As soon as dark entities take their last breath, Carrions actually jump on them, with the most loving of care, holding them tightly and securely but hurrying as fast as they can to the holding place. There's no stopping, no looking back, no hesitation of any kind. They're all business, and yet they do their jobs in a loving manner.

Francine says that everyone on the Other Side knows when Carrions are around because everything stops, like a "code blue" in a hospital when someone needs emergency resuscitation. If a dark entity has dropped or died, all the angels and guides step back and make a path for the Carrions to enter. If we were in the vicinity of a dark entity as it died, our angels would fold back. They might encompass us to protect us, but everything stops; everything becomes deadly still on the Other Side until the Carrions get that dark soul and whisk it away.

Carrions, by the way, are beautiful. They're not the dark little gnomes portrayed in movies. Their anima or totem is the raven, whose black color relates to the Carrions' function. Their element is the wind, a form of air that signifies the all-encompassing nature of their task: to allow no dark entities to escape. Their stone is the opal, and their wings are white with an orange tint.

When Francine told me about this phylum of angels, it gave me great peace to know that they carry away the evildoers so we don't have to see them on the Other Side. Please be aware, though, that in God's mercy, all entities play a part for our perfection. If there was no negative, we couldn't be assured that we would turn even more positive. If the dark entities aren't in a place of redemption, God absorbs them back into the uncreated mass. We, on the other hand, will always stay individual.

So many times people ask me if they, themselves, are dark or evil entities. The very fact that they ask this question shows that they're not dark or evil. If they were, they wouldn't ask. Dark entities never ask. They just seem to justify every mean and hateful thing they do without a trace of regret or remorse.

People also ask me about dark or evil spirits in their home or in their vicinity, but that's something else that just doesn't happen. It's either a manifestation of mental illness or possibly a confused, earthbound spirit who has died and doesn't know it and is, therefore, suicidal, aggravated, cranky, or mean. Such spirits can be terribly disruptive at times, but they really wish us no harm. They're simply *poltergeists,* a German word that means "mischievous spirit." I guess that's why I always say that we should be more afraid of the living than the dead.

Protection from Evil

I'm often asked, "Do angels come to us only when we ask for them?" The answer to that is no. Angels are always around us, but they do come and go, unlike our spirit guides who are always with us. Spirit guides have much more lateral movement than angels do. Guides can talk to each other, have parties together, and discuss us with each other and with the Council. Angels can't do these things. They're like wonderful missiles that are sent on particular duties and they don't deviate. You won't see a Power doing a Carrion's job, you won't see an Archangel doing what an Angel does, or an Angel picking up the green-orbed scepter of the Archangel. Just as a cat doesn't become a dog, angels don't disrupt their phyla. Their specific duties are relegated to them. So if you're in need of a healing, call on the Powers or the Archangels.

We each have our own angels, but when we call for additional angels to attend us, they will come—all, that is, except for the Carrions. We could ask for Carrions to come until we're blue in the face, but if we're white entities, they won't come near us. Why would they come when there's no reason for them to? Do they love us? Of course they do, but attending to us is not their job, unless we're dark entities, which *is* their job to deal with.

There is, however, one instance in which a white entity can call on the Carrions for help. If we want a dark entity to be kept away from us, we can call on the Carrions to blanket them from us. In those instances, they can protect us by surrounding the dark entity, not us, and negating its evil influences. I can't emphasize this enough. If we as white entities were surrounded by negativity, the Carrions would not come to us—they would go to the source of the negative energy. Carrions are totally allotted to the dark entities.

Calling on Angels for Healing

Years and years ago, in the time of early therapeutic hypnosis, magnetic force and electricity were involved. The pioneer of this type of therapy was a German physician named Franz Mesmer, whose name gave us the word *mesmerize.* Mesmer was one of the first to use water in conjunction with magnetic force and electricity. He had the right idea, but he almost electrocuted some of his patients and came close to being lynched in France because of it. True, he did effect healings, but his technique was archaic at best.

Fortunately, we don't have to resort to such methods. Instead, we can call on the Powers, with their blue electrical magnetic force. In fact, we can call on *all* the angels we've discussed so far and ask them to envelop us in a powerful healing circle—the Angels for protection, the Archangels with their healing scepters, the Cherubim and Seraphim with their joyous songs, and the Powers with their canopy of wings. When the Archangels touch our affected bodies with their healing scepters; when the Powers encompass us and emanate their healing energy; and when the Cherubim and Seraphim spiral upward in healing vibratory, tonal song, then tremendous healing forces are unleashed. You see, darkness can't live where music resounds. Darkness can't live where the power of God abounds. Darkness can't sustain itself. So, use the following meditation anytime you want to surround yourself with angels, and particularly if you're in need of healing.

MEDITATION FOR HEALING
(from Francine)

Put yourself in a comfortable, meditative position. Close your eyes. Relax your feet, your ankles, your calves, your knees, your thighs, and your buttocks area. Relax your body up through your trunk, arms, fingers, neck, and head, and feel now that your angels are beginning to gather.

Feel the first phylum, the Angels, beginning to come in for protection. Feel and sense the fluttering of wings as they gather about you in a protective barrier.

Now feel the Archangels starting to come in, large in stature and carrying their great batons with the green healing orbs at each end. Feel the sensation as they start to touch your body with their healing scepters, starting at the top of your head at the crown chakra and moving down the meridians of your body. Feel their touch as they tenderly tap the third-eye area in the middle of your forehead, moving downward past your eyes, nose, mouth, and throat area.

As they move downward with their healing batons, they may pause at a particular area for more effective healing. If they do, see the green orbs absorb the illness and negative energy, turning darker in the process. The Archangels now move down into your back and shoulder area, then your chest area, pausing at your solar plexus to cleanse that major chakra. Farther down they go with their healing scepters, through your stomach area; the trunk of your body; your reproductive organ area; and down into your legs, knees, ankles, and toes, cleansing as they go.

Now feel the Cherubim and Seraphim as they create a gigantic whirlpool of music around you. Their song, even if you don't hear it, will start filling up your cells with every single bit of their glorious tonal music and vibration. Each Cherubim and Seraphim knows your tone, so your body will resonate with this tone.

Now let us call on all the angels, emanating the energy of their totems and carrying their pearls, aquamarines, quartz, and emeralds. Call on the Powers, standing high with their large, beautiful wings. Now the Powers begin to surround you. They surround the room or area you are in, but they also surround your body as their wings unfold almost like a tent around you. Now they begin to emanate their electrical charge, and you see or sense the blue arcs of energy coming into your body. It does not hurt, but you begin to feel it cleansing, almost like an electrical charge that travels up and down your body, rinsing out any and all hurt, pain, anguish, suffering, viral infection, or disease. Feel the mending or rejuvenation of your vital organs.

The Powers now shift their wings. You sense the rustle of their wings and may even hear or feel a flapping noise as they do this. They now go into your cell memory and your subconscious mind, bringing forth memories of a past life or incident that may be causing illness or pain in your body. They make your mind and your bodily cells aware that this happened in your past and is no longer valid for this time and place. Experience this vision or impression, take it all in, and realize it for what it is. [If you are taping this for yourself, leave a blank space on your tape for this experience.]

Now release this past experience or illness as the energy of the Powers scrubs it clean from your mind and cells. Release it.

Now feel the warmth of the wings and a gentle breeze, so encompassed by God's love. Feel the beauty of this moment as the throngs and throngs of angels work over you, healing and protecting. They are sent from God to help you. Feel this electrical current playing around with your body. Give in to it. It will not hurt you, and you might be surprised if you feel a certain current in a part of your body that you did not know had any problem. Do not push it away; they know more than you do what your body needs, whether it is the lymphatic system, the endocrine gland system, the heart, the lungs. Let them loose on you, as we say.

Now feel the Powers slowly stand up and back away from you like sentinel figures. They fold their wings behind them and stand still, huge in stature and power. While they still stand about you, feel yourself come up, come up all the way back to full consciousness, feeling absolutely marvelous, better than you have ever felt before. On the count of three, bring yourself all the way up to full consciousness. One . . . two . . . three.

Use this meditation to work on any illness or sickness you may have. You can cut down on an illness, making it short term, short-lived, or ridding it completely from your body. If you feel improvement in any medical condition, please check with your physician for verification.

VI

The Virtues

"Whereas angels who are greater in might and power do not bring a reviling judgment against them before the Lord."

— 2 Peter 2:11

THE SEVENTH phylum of angels, the Virtues, are represented by the dove—signifying peace, love, and the Holy Spirit of communication from both Father and Mother God. Their stone, silver, is reflected in the color of their wings, whose pale blue tips give off a brilliant, silvery-blue luminescence. The Virtues' primary purpose is helping us with our charts, those blueprints for our lives here on Earth that we create on the Other Side before we're born into an incarnation. The element of the Virtues is water, signifying flexibility and change (which is what they do with our charts, if necessary).

In our charts, we choose our time of birth, our zodiac sign, our parents, our children and friends, our location on this earth, and the major events that relate to our themes (the areas we choose to perfect in this life)—and that's just the tip of the iceberg! Each of us usually has a primary theme and a secondary theme, which we've chosen from a list of 45 possibilities. These themes basically determine what our lives are about, and our lives revolve around them. I've included the following list of themes for your reference. Take a look at it and see if you can determine which two your own life falls under. (I don't want to go into greater detail here, as this material has been covered in my previous books, so to learn more about the themes and how they influence us, please read my book *Life on the Other Side,* published by Dutton.)

Life Themes

Activator	Humanitarian	Persecution
Aesthetic	Infallibility	Persecutor
Pursuits	Intellectuality	Poverty
Analyzer	Irritant	Psychic
Banner Carrier	Justice	Rejection
Builder	Lawfulness	Rescuer
Catalyst	Leader	Responsibility
Cause Fighter	Loner	Spirituality
Controller	Loser	Survival
Emotionality	Manipulator	Temperance
Experiencer	Passivity	Tolerance
Fallibility	Patience	Victim
Follower	Pawn	Victimizer
Harmony	Peacemaker	Warrior
Healer	Performer	Winner

On the Other Side, being in a state of bliss and wanting to perfect for God, we pick these courses of study. I know what you're thinking, because I've thought it, too: *What was wrong with me that I picked all this heartache in life? Why did I pick such a difficult theme?* What we sometimes don't understand is that just surviving our lives is enough. I truly believe that this life is the only hell we'll ever experience, and after we perfect here, our souls magnify the Lord. After many years, I've come to realize that without pain, as the old saying goes, there isn't any gain.

We all need help with perfecting our themes and carrying out our charts, because they're much more complicated than we may have realized. Our spirit guides, the Council, and our angels, especially the Virtues, are here to help us get the most out of this life that we can for God.

How the Virtues Help with Our Charts

On the Other Side, the Virtues primarily help us with our charts before we incarnate. Just before we enter this life, we go into isolation for meditation and a final review of what we want to accomplish. This is the time when the Virtues come to the foreground, helping us look over our charts one last time. No one disturbs us in this isolation process except for the Virtues, who you might say are the sentinels at the portals of entry into an incarnation. They're not involved with setting up our charts from the beginning; we do that with our spirit guides and the Council.

Rather, the Virtues help us review our charts one final time, just before we incarnate. It's a little like getting ready for a trip and having the opportunity to make last-minute changes. We might say, "Oh, I forgot to tell you to water the plants and feed the cat," or we might decide to skip or add an attraction on the trip to save time or because we'll be in the vicinity. We might not make big changes, but we may notice small, fine points that we had previously neglected.

The Virtues, unlike our spirit guides or any other phylum of angels, have the power to alter our charts without going to the Council for approval. In helping us get ready for our lives on Earth, the Virtues might ask, "Are you sure? Do you want to change anything? Do you want to tweak your chart? Do you want to elongate a certain area a little bit?" They wouldn't change any great, specific occurrences we've planned for our lives, such as deciding to meet someone who will have a profound effect on us, or having an accident that might injury us severely. No, the Virtues wouldn't add or delete any major points, but they certainly could modify them.

Let's take an accident, for instance. The greatest capability for modification is just before we incarnate, when we're still with the Virtues on the Other Side. It's at this time that we'd be more apt to say, "Okay, I did chart for an accident where I wanted to have my leg broken, because I really needed to rest and didn't know how else to accomplish it. But I've changed my mind and have decided I don't need that much rest. Instead, I'll only sprain my ankle."

In other words, we can modify the event—without changing the actual action—by changing a minor part of it. Maybe we change the pain level, or the length of time we need to recover, but we don't eliminate the accident completely or take away the opportunity to get some much-needed rest.

Here's another example of how the Virtues can help us adjust our charts. Let's say I'd planned to have an IQ of 120 for a particular life. Then subsequently I decided that for the work I intended to do, I'd need an IQ of 145 or 150. The Virtues, upon reviewing my chart with me, might even argue that I'll need an IQ of 160 to complete my life's task. With love for our well-being and success, the Virtues will argue or discuss their recommended changes with us, and then make the adjustment. The Virtues are the last creation of God that we normally see before we incarnate, and they communicate both Father and Mother God's love for us as we begin our journey.

Modifying a Chart Here on Earth

As I said, the greatest opportunity for modifying our charts occurs before incarnation, but we can also modify the occurrence later, while we're in life. The following story illustrates what I mean.

Valerie writes:

"I truly believe to this day that my life was changed by an angel in human form. It happened in March of 1996 on the island of Gozo, near Malta. The events that transpired after this first meeting changed my life forever.

"I was in my shop on a windy afternoon. I was on the telephone when I saw a man and woman enter. I saw the man leave but not the woman, who stayed. She was beautiful in an angelic way and had a regal bearing. She approached me, and we began to converse about my shop. She then quite abruptly asked me if I knew what a 'medium' was. I answered yes, and told her I'd never been with a medium or psychic before. I suddenly found myself asking her if she could help me. She answered, 'That is why I have come.'

"For the next hour, she proceeded to tell me about my life and what terrible danger I was in. She gave me messages from relatives who had passed on, and she confirmed all my worst fears. She also gave me hope and guidance, which was like no other since. It's from this meeting that my spirit was rekindled, and I began the long road to regain control of my life, and in so doing, left behind the evil that had permeated it. During this time, no other person came into the shop. When I commented about it, she said, 'Of course they wouldn't have; I was working to help save you.' When I asked her how she came to me that particular day, her answer was: 'God always sends me where I am most needed.' I know I was saved that day, and by a complete stranger."

The angel that Valerie described obviously had great knowledge of her chart. Unlike many of the angel stories contained in this book, the woman in the shop appeared to speak with a human voice rather than through telepathic contact that seemed real. In this instance, information about Valerie's chart may have been passed from a Virtue to Valerie's spirit guide, or another angel who took human form to deliver the message. It really doesn't matter, though; ultimately, the message comes from an all-loving God.

A Welcoming Party on the Other Side

Normally, the Virtues don't descend or appear here on Earth. Their function is to help us on the Other Side before we come into this life. However, they (as well as the Dominions and some of the other phyla) will meet us at the end of the tunnel when we return to the Other Side. Sometimes they even line the tunnel, and Francine reports that she's seen them come as far down as two-thirds of the way to greet a returning soul. Virtues usually line the tunnel when a person of great spiritual ability passes over—not because the person is so elevated, but to show respect for the entity and what he or she has gone through in life.

Virtues are the only phyla who form a line in the tunnel, where their bright, luminous glow helps provide some of the light people often describe. Once we get through the tunnel, though, we'll see Thrones, Principalities, Dominions, and all the other angel phyla.

Melissa writes about an angel who brought peace in a vision and stood by while her grandmother passed:

"I've had an experience, but I'm not sure it was an angel. When my grandmother passed, I had some sort of vision or something. I saw my grandmother lying down, with a woman standing over her with a broad smile and a flowing white gown or dress. Everything was beautifully white. The woman didn't say anything, just smiled, and I knew that everything was okay. What peace that brought to my heart and mind after seeing that beautiful sight."

A similar letter came from Pat, who writes:

"I would like to tell you of a conversation between my mother and her friend. My mother phoned me one morning, very excited. She told me of a woman who was beside her bed throughout the night. She said that the beauty and love she had seen in this person's face were almost indescribable. She told me that she knew it was an angel. My mother was very ill at the time. She said that the angel didn't move her lips; however, she said my mother would be okay and she needed to be strong.

"A few days later, my mother was talking to her friend and asked her if she had ever dreamed of angels, because my mother strongly believed she did. Her friend replied that she had, that there was a group of them around her bed as she lay there a few nights ago. She said they were magnificent and beautiful. I looked at both women, and they had a look of peace around them. That would be the last time we would see her friend, as she passed away three days later. She even said to me that she would see me on Wednesday. I did see her Wednesday . . . at her funeral.

"Back to my mother. She had heart problems and was very ill for a long time. The unexpected death of her friend and her twin sister two months later, I believe, was what the angel was trying to tell my mother about having strength and that she wasn't alone. My mother suffered with her illness for many years and had lost all her friends, including the last two who couldn't have been any closer to her. She was alone; however, I believe that angel was with her right up to the time she passed away 15 months later."

Angels do come to give solace, comfort, and the knowledge that people survive on the Other Side. Rest assured that Pat's mother and her friends and loved ones are all well and happy on the Other Side, and that their angels greeted them warmly when they arrived. We will all share that experience someday. Meanwhile, when we need help with our charts or with a particular problem, illness, or difficult situation, we can use the following meditation to call upon the Virtues for help.

MEDITATION FOR HELP WITH OUR CHARTS, AND IN TIMES OF TROUBLE

Sit or lie in a comfortable, meditative position. Close your eyes. Relax your feet, your ankles, your calves, your knees, your thighs, and your buttocks area. Relax your body up through your trunk, arms, fingers, neck, and head. Take three deep breaths, surround yourself with a golden light, and pray the following prayer.

Dearest Mother, please send your angels to help me _____ [state petition], so that I will fulfill my chart, but I ask for Your intercession in this time of sickness, despair, grief, or hopelessness. Let Your angels come and watch over me. Remove all pain and suffering and help me to see the light out of this dark tunnel, and to give me health and insight into my life.

Lie there and contemplate not only the problem, but also the positive outcome. The angels will stand around your bed and protect you from all harm.

Bring yourself up or, even better, let yourself go to sleep.

VII

The Dominions

*"And most surely there are keepers
over you Honorable recorders.
They know what you do."*

— Koran 82:10–12

THE DOMINIONS, the eighth phylum of angels, oversee our good deeds and actions and record them on a permanent chart known as the Akashic record. Every person since the beginning of time has his or her own individual Akashic record. These, in turn, make up the huge Akashic record for all of creation. Some people call this their book, or their private scroll; I prefer the term *Book of Life*. Whatever title we may choose, it's important to know that all of our actions and deeds are recorded and maintained by the Dominions.

You might wonder how in the world one book could possibly be big enough. There's no way to explain how a single volume could be large enough to contain all the records of creation, but Francine assures us that there definitely is one that does so. She compares it to the principle that says 100 angels can sit on the head of a pin. On the Other Side, time, space, and physics are not the same as they are here; there are no limitations to time or space.

The Dominions are one of the busiest of angel phyla, and they're the most elite as far as studiousness is concerned. They're sort of the intelligentsia of all the angels. Their totem is the cougar, which signifies their strength and dignity. Their element is earth, which represents grounding and the lives they record, and their stone is the bloodstone. Symbolizing the blood of life, it matches their wings, which are white with a tinted maroon color.

How Dominions Help Our Guides

Dominions help our guides in two different ways. First, they have the ability to determine which phylum of angels can provide the most help for a particular problem, and they're always right. Second, they have ongoing access to our charts and can instantly answer any question our guides may have.

Dominions have the power to enlist the aid of minions of angels with a snap of their fingers, but our guides are the ones who call on the different phyla of angels to help us through bad situations. It's not that the guides are ever looked upon as being lower than the Dominions. In fact, put to the test—and they don't mind my saying this—a guide will overrule an angel any day. Our spirit guides always take precedence, because they have a much better overall picture of us and have also lived on our plane. Their humanization helps them better understand us. Angels, on the other hand, have never incarnated into this plane. Although they're pure love, they're often more focused on their own created purpose. They have specific duties on the Other Side and are not humanized to the extent that our guides are.

The Dominions, like the Virtues, don't normally

descend into our plane of existence. They don't move laterally on the Other Side very well, either, as most of the time they confine themselves to their own particular quadrant. Again, to elaborate on the term *quadrants* for those who may not have read my previous books, bear with me while I briefly explain a little more about them.

As you learned earlier in this book, on the Other Side all the geographic masses that we humans have here on Earth are duplicated, except for the ocean areas, which aren't quite as large. Each of our continents is duplicated and divided into four distinct areas or quadrants. What you may not realize is that this division into quadrants serves a unique purpose: It's designed for specialization among the different occupations of entities on the Other Side. In other words, animal husbandry might take place in one quadrant, research in another, and teaching in still another.

Here on Earth, no matter which area of the world we may live in, it falls into one of these quadrants. The Dominions are each assigned to a particular quadrant, and they're responsible for recording the lives of all the entities who live within that quadrant. Dominions have complete interaction with each other, so if we travel or move to a different area, the Dominions in the new quadrant simply take over our record keeping.

Like the Council, Dominions have a great deal of access to our life's charts. The Dominions are the bearers of information, which they feed directly to any spirit guides who might need extra help in guiding their charges. As a matter of protocol, guides will sometimes go to the Dominions rather than directly to the Council in garnering this help. Sometimes a guide may not want to bother the Council with some minor detail, although Francine says she's gone to the Dominions with major issues, too.

Certainly if she's worried about something, she goes directly to the Council, but if there's something that needs to be updated or something she doesn't know about, she can go to the Dominions and ask what she should do. Spirit guides go to the Dominions for extra help with all different types of questions, including financial, health, relationships, and a myriad of other problems. Since the Dominions are the keepers of our records and charts, they can often offer help with a particular situation.

Even though our guides know our charts, things can sometimes go awry. We may be involved in impending danger or urgent circumstances in which the guide doesn't have time to scroll through all the specifics of our individual records. Frankly, our charts can be quite laborious to go through—kind of like reading a telephone book. They're loaded with minute details and little innuendos, and if the guide is in a hurry, there may not be time to sift through it all. In those instances, the guide can run to the Dominions for an instantaneous answer to any question. If the guide just wants to see the outcome, he or she can ask, "What's the outcome for this person? Is this the exit point? Is my charge in danger?" Since our spirit guides consult them frequently, Dominions keep our individual records close at hand. Armed with answers from the Dominions, the guides can then become what I call "nudging spirits," infiltrating our minds and helping us get on the right track.

This intricate arrangement is better than any security system I've ever seen. It surpasses even the most sophisticated intelligence organization or decoding process. If something disrupts our charts, our guides do as much as they can to renovate or seek alternate means to get us back on our chosen path.

Sometimes they get a little myopic because they're so busy with the moment. When that happens, they have to stop, even though they have wonderful memories, and get themselves constantly adjusted and readjusted to our charts. Our relationship with our guides is much like a love affair. They get caught up in what they want for us, and they can even get overly emotional when we experience hurt and pain. Because they are sort of half in and half out of our dimension, they absorb negativity from being involved in *our* negativity. As a result, they periodically require a type of cleansing, which is done by the Council. If they weren't humanized to a certain extent, they would be of no service to us. Are they elevated? Yes. Are they sanctified? Absolutely. But they have to relate to what we go through in life in order to help us.

The Orientation Process

As I stated earlier, the Dominions record our deeds, especially the good ones. This task is quite useful to us, because their records help us immensely when we return to the Other Side.

When we cross over from this life, we go through a tunnel toward a brilliant white light. For most of us, the process is familiar; we've done it many times because we've lived many lives. Upon arrival, we exit the tunnel and greet our loved ones, guides, and angels who await us. On the Other Side, everyone is happy and filled with the peacefulness, joy, and bliss that Father and Mother God provide. When one of us returns to the Other Side, we immediately feel this wonderful atmosphere of happiness.

After the initial celebration of returning Home, we go to either the Hall of Justice or the Hall of Wisdom (two spectacular buildings on the Other Side) to review our just-completed life on the Earth plane. This process is called *orientation.* Everyone goes through the orientation process when they return from an incarnation. During orientation, we review the life we've lived, and we become reoriented to the Other Side. We usually do this with the help of our guides, master teachers, or counselors.

We view our lives on what Francine calls a "scanner," which is much like a television in the sense that we can see and hear ourselves and others. Unlike a TV set, the scanner lets us view any time period in the life we've just lived.

We can view our actions, reactions, and the myriad of emotions we experienced in life. We decide what we want to review and at what pace we want to review it. The choice is entirely up to us, and we're the ones who judge our lives. Contrary to popular belief, no one on the Other Side judges us. We're the ones who applaud or abrade ourselves, if we so choose.

At this point, the purpose of the Dominions comes very much into play. The Dominions, being the record keepers, have written down the events of our lives, concentrating on our good deeds and acts. These acts are recorded in gold on a beautiful scroll, one scroll for each of us. Our scrolls are private and aren't brought out for the populace to view. Often, during the orientation process, we may begin abrading ourselves. It's then that our beautiful scrolls are brought out and we're told, "So, you think you're so bad. Look at all the good things you did."

This reminder of our good deeds helps us a great deal, especially when we're feeling grief or guilt. I don't know of one human being—unless they're just totally off the chart, with their ego out of whack—who doesn't come into orientation without some feelings of regret. With few exceptions, people almost always say, "I could have done, I should have done, or I wish I had done." It's the Dominions, with their records of good actions, who help prevent us from becoming too traumatized, by saying, "Look, this is what you've done; this is your positive record." These positive records kept by the Dominions help us put our lives in perspective so we can learn from our negative experiences and enrich our souls with that knowledge.

Heralds of Incoming Souls

There's a great multitude of Dominions, more than enough to record the lives of every entity on Earth. The Dominions are also what we might call the "heralds of incoming souls." They stand at the end of the tunnel and form a gateway of welcome for those souls who pass over. When people see angels coming, such as in deathbed situations or even astral trips, they're more than likely seeing Dominions.

Sheila from North Carolina writes:

"I was blessed with the sight of an entire host of angels that came to escort my husband, Butch, from this world. We were both only 25 years old at the time, but he'd been diagnosed with a very rare disease akin to leukemia. After the diagnosis, he lived much longer than the medical professionals expected and was a willing participant in any new experimental treatment his doctors wanted to try. After his passing, I gave his doctors permission to use his case history in medical journals. That was 20 years ago.

"After another emergency surgery, Butch was sent home to spend his last days. The doctors could do no more, so his passing was expected. The night he left, I was sleeping in a chair beside the hospital bed that the hospice had provided. My alarm was set to wake me every two hours to administer medication. I was awakened at an unscheduled time. I knew it was time for him to go. Although I was sad that it was time for him to leave, I was happy that he would no longer have to suffer in that body.

"He seemed to be sleeping, but was having trouble breathing. I really didn't know what to do, so I just reached over, took his hand, closed my eyes, and whispered, 'I'm here.' Then, just as I opened my eyes again, a perfect circle of angels appeared, surrounding us. They formed a rather large circle around the bed. The bed was situated against a wall, but it was as if the walls weren't even there. Although I could only see the angels that were in the room with us, I knew that the circle extended through the walls. The angels seemed very large and were hovering about three feet off the floor. They were clothed in white robes with gold trim, and I could see the outline of wings behind them, but they didn't look like the typical angels we normally see in pictures. I could see no facial features, only light, and there was glowing light all around them.

The sight of the angels could have lasted no more than a split second, but it was a sight I'll never forget. Although they came for Butch, it was a comfort to me that they allowed me to see them, also."

Angels are always with us, and when we pass over, they help us make it to the Other Side. As you learned in the last chapter, the Virtues line the tunnel, but the Dominions await us at its end—the first angels to greet us on the Other Side.

PRAYER TO LESSEN THE FEAR OF DEATH

Dearest Virtues and Dominions, when I get ready to go Home, please be in attendance to help me cross the barrier between life and the eternal blessed true life hereafter. Do not let me live my life in fear of crossing to the Other Side. Stay with me in this life, and help me be unafraid, knowing you are always standing like central figures of protection. Amen.

MEDITATION FOR ANGELS TO SURROUND YOU

Sit or lie in a comfortable, meditative position. Close your eyes. Relax your feet, your ankles, your calves, your knees, your thighs, and your buttocks area. Relax your body up through your trunk, arms, fingers, neck, and head.

Be relaxed. See the tunnel of light. See the glorious angels standing in attendance. You can even will yourself to astrally project to the Other Side. Feel that each time you pass these glorious entities, you are filled with peace, light, courage, and love. If you get to the Other Side, look around and validate what so many have seen. Then bring yourself back to yourself, feeling unafraid. More important, feel that life, while very precious, is only a learning place.

VIII

The Thrones and Principalities

"Bless the Lord, all ye His angels: you that are mighty in strength, and execute His word, hearkening to the voice of His orders. Bless the Lord, all ye His hosts: you ministers of His that do His will."

— Psalm 103:20–21

AFTER ALL the angels we've explored, we come at last to the final two categories. No phyla are superior to the Thrones and Principalities. They're truly Mother and Father God's armies, and they're by far the highest, most elevated, and most spiritual of all the angels. Some religions have almost deified the Archangels. It isn't wrong to do so, but it's erroneous. No angels have higher powers than the Thrones and Principalities. I call on them less frequently, maybe because I've always felt that we should keep the best for last or when we feel that we're in the most danger.

Even in Biblical texts, more so than with many of the other categories of angels, the Thrones and Principalities are mentioned with great care and awe. In Ezekiel 1:13, their appearance is described as "like burning coals of fire."

The Thrones and Principalities are usually sent when danger is imminent or when we feel impending mental, physical, emotional, or even psychic harm. They are also most definitely the protectorates of children and animals. When I've worked for the Make-A-Wish Foundation® (which I dearly love), I always call on the Principalities and Thrones to protect my loved ones, everyone in danger, and especially the children.

We should never hesitate to call on the Thrones and Principalities in our darkest hours, or when we need guidance. Mother and Father God will send them anyway, but as stated earlier, our belief in them and our willingness to call upon them help pierce the veil between this lower vibration of Earth and the higher vibration of the Other Side.

The Thrones belong to Azna, the Mother God, while the Principalities belong to Om, the Father God. The Principalities will come if we call for them, but they're really the "guardians of the gate," the guardians around Father God. Like Him, they're static, stately, and sentinel. The Thrones, like Azna, are much more active.

Mother God's Army: The Thrones

The ninth phylum on the angel chart, the Thrones, are the fighters among the angel phyla. They're Azna's army, and like Her, they carry a sword. If we think that only Azna comes when we call Her, we're very much mistaken. Francine says that she doesn't think she's ever seen Azna come to our aid without a group or a minion of Thrones in tow. They trail to the sides of Her, in front of Her, in back of Her—all around Her.

Azna has control of, or is the central figure of, all the angels. Wherever Azna goes, angels follow. The Thrones are Her babies—you might say, Her army—and they'll always be with Her regardless of how many other angels are present. She doesn't utilize the Principalities much, as they're designated to Father God, but Azna has been known to have Archangels, Virtues, Angels, and all the other phyla accompanying Her. She's even been known to get the Carrions to come with Her. She utilizes them to surround dark entities to negate their influence. As I said in an earlier chapter, we also can utilize Carrions in this manner if we call on them to help us.

Azna is the one who deals with negativity in creation, and the Thrones help Her fight and banish the darkness. Francine uses the analogy of Joan of Arc to describe Azna. Being pure emotion, Azna uses Her army of Thrones to follow behind Her, brandishing their swords to cut through darkness. Azna is known as the emotional Mother God, protecting Her creations like a mother protects her children. The Thrones emanate this same quality and are active in fighting against negative energy and entities. They're very powerful, and no darkness can stand against them. Their anima is the elephant, which relates to their size as well as to the protective aspect of elephants to their young. Their element is air, which is all-encompassing and found everywhere. Their stone is gold, again relating to purity and royalty; and their wings are purplish white, the color of royalty and power.

The following letter from JoAnn describes the powerful protection offered by Azna and Her angels:

"My story starts with my mother and sister going to pick up my father one rainy night. They were driving down a heavily traveled road when a man ran a red light and rammed into the car on the driver's side. The impact was so severe that it broke the steering wheel off into my mother's stomach and slammed my sister into the dashboard. The emergency assistance people brought in the Jaws of Life, to no avail. Just then, a man came out of nowhere, put his hand on the door handle, and opened that door like it had never been stuck. My mother saw him and could have identified him except for the fact that he was nowhere to be found. They advertised in the paper and in and around the bases here to find him, but . . . nothing. Had it not been for him, my mother and sister would have surely perished.

"My other angel story is a personal one. I used to be a real wild thing (I worked through it, thank goodness). I'd gone to a bar with a friend, and when it came time to go home, my friend was in the process of hooking up with a girl, so he said that *his* friend would drive me home. To say the least, I thought I would die before I got home, since he was extremely drunk. I talked him into pulling over and letting me drive the rest of the way home. It was about 2:00 or 2:30 A.M., and all I wanted to do was get home safe.

"Well, I got all the way to my street, and he reached his foot over and slammed on the brakes, ripped my dress open, and tried to force himself on me. I was screaming my head off. Just then, a young man opened the door, grabbed my arm, yanked me out, and told me to run home. I could hear him gaining control over this madman, so I ran like hell and didn't look back. You have to realize that I lived in a not-very-busy place where no one ever walked around at 2:00 A.M., let alone on a Sunday night, so this was truly amazing."

Angels have the strength to put out fires, help us in times of great physical danger, and also—what we often fail to realize—in times of emotional distress. Divorce, loss of loved ones . . . no category of life is too complicated for an angel to tackle.

Father God's Army: The Principalities

The Bible refers to the Principalities as those in charge of nations and great cities. It even calls them the protectors of religion or spirituality, and says that they've been known to escort people to heaven. All religions seem to agree that the higher the phylum, the more grace and power it comes with, to give us particular solace in whatever area we need. Regardless of whether the

Principalities are portrayed as protectors or as being as strong as fire, this highest phylum is described as having great power and being close to the throne of God. These portrayals bear up what Francine has stated: The higher the phylum of angels, the greater the magnitude of their jobs. That doesn't mean that we can't all call on them, it just bears witness to the delineation of their "job descriptions."

The anima of Father God's army is the lion, appropriately symbolic as the king of beasts. The element of the Principalities is fire, which is one of the most powerful cleansing elements. Their stone is sapphire, which has always been linked with royalty, and their wings are gold, which has always been considered one of the most precious of metals and is associated with kings.

Principalities are known to have high intelligence, and they carry golden spears. Without much movement, they can send their powers outward. Unlike the Thrones, who come with Azna in minions or throngs, Francine says that she rarely sees large groups of Principalities. They're more likely to come and stand as sentinel figures around us, in small groups of two or three. They seem to be static in nature, standing silently rather than moving with agility. Francine says they're sometimes mistaken for statues. Like the guards of an English king or queen, they can't be made to smile or smirk.

When we had our terrible disaster at the World Trade Center, Francine says the Principalities were standing near Ground Zero. No one saw how they got there, but the

Principalities stood guard like golden statues, immobile and emanating tremendous power. Azna was there, too, with all her minions of Thrones brandishing their swords, cutting off all darkness, and helping those who had died get over to the Other Side.

Whenever there's a disaster, such as the terrible 1999 earthquake that killed thousands of people in Turkey, the Principalities seem to appear as sentinels, or guardian figures. The other phyla may rush around, fighting darkness, doing, helping, picking up, carrying messages, but not the Principalities. They reflect Om, the Father God, in the sense of almost sustaining a protective energy in which other angels can go about the business at hand.

Most people seem to think of the Principalities as being more relegated to disasters and emanating protective, sustaining energy, but please don't think that means we shouldn't call on them for other reasons. They'll always come to stand around us. Francine says that when we call on any of the angels, she's never seen them fail to come. But if we call on the Principalities, we might get one or two, even if we're in what we might call a disaster period. They're more like guardians of the world, whereas we're more likely to be helped individually by most of the other phyla, such as the Archangels with their scepters, the Carrions who take away dark entities, or the Cherubim and Seraphim who fill our souls with music.

The Principalities may stand still, but don't ever mistake their emanation as not being powerful; their power is immeasurable. One Principality can knock out and protect us from thousands and thousands of dark entities or any force of negativity around us. Nevertheless, we shouldn't feel slighted if we call on the Principalities and they don't come rushing in right away. It's not because they don't love us, but their primary function is to attend Father God and be His army. Just as soldiers wouldn't desert their king, the Principalities wouldn't rush to us and leave God unattended. It isn't that God the Father isn't strong enough to attend to Himself, but the Principalities are a divine creation that was centered on God the Father. They're magnificent and brilliant, but they do serve Him.

If God the Father takes on any presence, He chooses not to hold it for any length of time. Francine says that sometimes the only way she can tell He's present is when the Principalities assemble, almost like a silhouette filled in by God. She has seen His visage, but only briefly because it just has too much power.

The angel story that follows reveals God's loving awareness. This feeling, so prominent in the thousands of stories of love and caring from all over the world, can't just be a fantasy. Aside from being separated by time, locale, and age, all the angel stories I've received share a common denominator: *love.* Whether we're believers, skeptics, or people who just aren't sure, we must realize that all of these stories were written by people like you and me—most with no preconceived notion that they were going to encounter an angel, let alone be helped by one. Maybe, just maybe, God in His eternal love for us sends His help in many ways, with angels being just one manifestation of that love and help.

Dixie writes:

"I think an angel saved our lives. About 12 years ago, I'd just picked my mom up from work. We were getting off the ramp to go back on the freeway when we hit a patch of ice. I lost control of the car, and it ended up doing a 180-degree turn on the busy freeway. Miraculously, we stopped inches from hitting the barrier. We were facing the traffic head-on, and somehow no cars hit us. My mom and I were very frightened. After waiting for a clear spot to turn around, we pulled off the side of the road and started breathing again. My mom decided that she should drive home, so on the way there I was looking out the window and I could see something. It was white with massive wings, and it was flying up in a tunnel of light. I thought I was hallucinating. I think it was an angel that saved us on that winter night."

It did, Dixie, because you're not given to fantasy and never have been.

MEDITATION FOR PROTECTION AND REMOVAL OF NEGATIVITY

Sit or lie in a comfortable, meditative position. Close your eyes. Relax your feet, your ankles, your calves, your knees, your thighs, and your buttocks area. Relax your body up through your trunk, arms, fingers, neck, and head.

Surround yourself with a white, purple, and gold light. Ask Mother God Azna to send in the Thrones to protect and watch over you and yours. See their golden lights and colors emanating from their wings. See them with their swords cutting away all darkness and adversity (the sword is Azna's symbol; notice how the sword makes a cross). Feel the peace and joy descend right from the top of your head to the tips of your toes.

Now ask Om, the Father God, to send the Principalities—an army of beauty, but more steadfast and static. They stand much like the Virtues and Dominions, as sentinel figures, but nothing can penetrate the barrier of their love and protection.

Surround your loved ones and yourself at least once a week, or if in dire straits, once a day. No angel gets tired of being called.

IX

Frequently Asked Questions

"O Lord! Assist those who have renounced all else but Thee, and grant them a mighty victory. Send down upon them, O Lord, the concourse of the angels in heaven and earth and all that is between, to aid Thy servants, to succour [sic] and strengthen them, to enable them to achieve success, to sustain them, to invest them with glory, to confer upon them honour and exaltation, to enrich them and to make them triumphant with a wondrous triumph."

— The Báb, *Selections from the Writings of the Báb*

OVER THE years, I've received thousands of wondrous angel stories and many often-asked questions. No tome would be big enough to hold them all, so I've decided to use the last two chapters of this book to share a few more of them with you. In this chapter, I'm going to focus on some questions and answers I've researched. Some of these questions may seem simple, and some have been answered previously, but here, I go into them in even more depth.

Q: How should I address an angel? Should I use any special words or say a specific prayer?

A: There is no special way to call upon an angel. Just say, "I want an angel for protection" (or healing or whatever). Think it, and they'll be there. Merely uttering the word *angels* gets them to your side. Not only that, but the correct angel for the problem will come. Francine says that even guides have sometimes called on one sector of angels that they thought a person needed, and another group of angels came instead. For example, she's called on an Archangel for me and gotten a Virtue or a Throne. She never questions it, though, because she realizes that angels know the vibrational level of the person they're dealing with more than spirit guides or humans do. I'm talking about direct reports from God. So, our vibrational level calls upon the correct angel. I've gotten to the point these days that I just say, "Whatever angel is needed, get them in here."

Q: Do angels have bodies like we do?

A: Angels have real bodies, but they're on a higher vibration, so it's often difficult for them to take form. Often, though, as we've seen in the previous stories, they can take human form for a short time and then seem to disappear.

Q: Do angels speak to us, and if so, how?

A: Angels speak telepathically when they're in "angel form," and often seemingly in words when they briefly take human form.

Q: How can I contact my angels or a particular phylum of angels?

A: The meditations in this book will help, but many times it's simply a matter of asking for assistance. Refer to the previous chapters for the specific tasks each phylum performs (such as "healer" or "protector"), and call upon that phylum. For example, Archangels can be called on for healing, and Virtues can be called on for assistance with our charts.

Q: Are passed loved ones ever angels?

A: No, angels are a specific species or phylum. When we pass, we can be spirit guides, because we've had lives, but angels never have to live lives because they don't have the lessons to learn that we do.

Q: What's the difference between spirit guides and angels?

A: This answer is similar to the previous one. Angels were made as companions and protectors to humanity. Spirit guides, on the other hand, have lived lives in order to perfect. The chance that we will be or have been a spirit guide is 100 percent.

Q: Do angels have names?

A: Many of the religious texts give names to the angels, but that seems to be more of a dogmatic human thing. We can call them any name, but personally I feel it's just as important to call on the specific phylum we need. However, when in doubt, call on *all* of them.

Q: Does everyone have a guardian angel?

A: Yes, everyone has a guardian angel, except for dark, evil entities. These entities seem to be alone without any direction, and they don't seem to want it. I'm sure these dark entities are manipulated by evil, and they don't have spirit guides or angels as we do.

Q: Is Satan a fallen angel?

A: Logically, why would there just be one entity with horns and a tail? Satan is not just one single being, but a group of entities who separated from God in the beginning. They weren't angels, because there's no such thing as evil angels. This would be an oxymoron, rebutting the word *angel.* All angels are good, pure, created life forms whose only will is to serve God. We humans, on the other hand, because we're on a mission to learn for God, in the beginning chose either wrong (the dark side) or right (white entities). This, however, never refers to color of skin; the dark and white aspect refers only to the soul.

This Earth plane is the only hell we will endure, and this is where the dark entities seem to survive; but with God's army of angels, spirit guides, the Holy Spirit, and the Christ consciousness, white entities will always overcome evil, even if at times they seem to be losing. Ultimately, what goes around comes around.

Q: Why do angels have wings?

A: I've thought about this a lot, and with the help of my own research and spirit guide communication, as well as people under hypnosis (which, by the way, can provide a wealth of valid information), I believe the purpose of their wings is to differentiate them from the other entities, such as loved ones who have passed over, spirit guides, and so on. It seems to be their badge. Also, consider what was briefly mentioned in the chapters before. Their wings symbolize how fast they can move and also the comfort of knowing they can protect and enfold us in their love.

Q: Do angels come in different sizes or guises?

A: Yes, some angels can make themselves very large, especially the Thrones and Principalities. They can also be shorter, even to being just inches tall; but in all of my research, contrary to many artists' renderings, there are no children or baby angels. They can also, as we've seen in the preceding chapters, take on human form for a short time to protect or warn us. Many religions still believe we should be kind to strangers because they could be angels in disguise. I hate to be a wet blanket, but in today's world, while good deeds are so needed, we also have to be a little more discerning.

Q: Do angels have personalities?

A: I would be more inclined to say that they have definite personas, given their different levels and what they're best suited for (healing, singing, protection, and so on). No, I've never heard of a group of angels having a get-together on the Other Side or telling jokes like we do. They seem to be a form of intelligence with a serenity and singular purpose, who ask for nothing in return.

Q: Are angels independent, or must they act only if God tells them to?

A: Angels seem to not only know where God wants them to go, but they're always watching over us. Our spirit guides also play a part in calling angels, but don't ever think we don't have the power to call them ourselves—and we should, like I do every day. The two groups that seem to be directly sent from God are the Principalities and Thrones. We could call them on our own, but we first go to Mother and Father God, then angels, guides, loved ones, and so on.

Q: Do Father God and Mother God sit on thrones, and if so, do angels sit by Them?

A: Father God Om and Mother God Azna do not have thrones. This image was more or less constructed by humans, who seem to want to humanize God as if He/She were a king or queen. God is everywhere and in everything, but both Mother and Father God have a definite entity structure. The only thing I've learned from research is that, while God the Father is a male entity, He is too powerful and chooses to hold a form for only a short length of time. Mother Azna, on the other hand, takes a form almost all the time and can be everywhere. The angels don't sit near any nonexistent throne; they, too, are everywhere. They're around the world, around us, around our houses, at work—everywhere.

Q: Why do the angel phyla have different names and duties?

A: Angels within the phyla don't have individual names, although many religious writings give them humanized names such as Michael, Raphael, and Ariel. In truth, they're not defined that individually. They respond to the name of their particular phylum. If you want heavenly music, call on the Cherubim and Seraphim. If you want healing, call on the Archangels or Powers.

Q: Why did God create angels? Aren't we enough for Him?

A: Of course we're enough for God, but God, being all-knowing, realized that we'd need protectorates here on Earth and its sometimes hellish environment. Hence, He created the angels.

Q: How many angels are there?

A: Every religious text, along with people who have experienced the Other Side, relates or states the same premise: There seem to be legions of angels, more than anyone can count. My guide says that no one has ever counted them, but they seem to be in the trillions. This makes sense, and at any given time we can have five or six (or legions of) angels around us when we're in need. It bears mentioning that angels also protect the earth and all the animals.

Q: Why do some religions portray angels as warriors or avengers who rise up against those who defy God and His teachings?

A: This is all a fantasy. It goes back to the erroneous belief that God is mean and spiteful. If that were true, then God would be vengeful. But God, being all love, never sends anyone to hurt another person, place, or thing, and He certainly wouldn't send an angel to do so. God can't be all love and still take sides. Of course, Angels are protectorates, and they, like the Thrones, carry swords, but that's only to cut through the darkness of negativity.

Q: Why do guides need angels? Don't they have enough power?

A: Of course they do, but why not call on all the troops, as it were, to help the entities they guide? Many times Francine has told me that spirit guides are always attended to by angels when watching out for us. I guess, simply stated, more is better. Realize, also, that guides do more than just give love and protection like angels. They need angels to help them in their vigilance while they attend to other matters in our charts.

Q: If angels have so much power, why can't they always help us?

A: I'm sorry to say that this question sometimes really frustrates me. It's no one's fault; I just wish more people were aware that without angels, we'd be in really dire straits. I'd just like everyone to look over their lives and try to relive memories of those times when they could have almost died or had a serious accident or felt warned about a certain situation. Let's get the words *coincidence* and *imagination* out of our vocabulary. If you kept a journal for just one week, recording how many times you received messages or feelings, you'd never doubt the verbalization from your guides, or the unseen but nevertheless real presence of angels in your life.

Angels can't always help us by changing our charts that we contracted with God to learn, but they can certainly make the journey easier by giving us courage to face our lives, or warning us so we don't take a wrong exit point. I truly know that life would be far more dark and desolate without them.

This next question may seem strange, but I've heard it so many times that I'm convinced it fits under the category of curses or possession. Of course we can't ever be cursed or possessed, but here goes:

Q: Do angels kill people for God?

A: What a paradox this would be. Angels are here out of love, caring, and protection, and it would be against their very essence of goodness to hurt or kill. So the answer is a resounding *no!*

Q: Why don't angels manifest more often to us?

A: They do, but we're not always aware of the messages they give us, whether it's a message from a stranger or sparkles of light at night, the wisp of a feather, or a tele-pathic message.

Right after I wrote this last answer, I was in a small boutique. A lovely dark-haired woman stood behind the counter. She smiled and asked if she could help me. I said, "No, thanks, I'm just looking." I looked around and decided the shop was a little pricey, so I turned to leave and thanked her.

She said, "Please take care of yourself. So many people need you." I stood there a moment and stared at her.

Being gutsy, I asked, "Do you know me?" thinking she had seen me on TV.

She said, "Not in the way you think I know you." I was a little shaken, which is unusual for me.

Later, after telling my daughter-in-law about the

encounter, we went back to the shop. This time, a large-boned, blonde woman stood behind the counter. I asked her about the lovely, dark-haired woman who had been there earlier in the day.

The blonde woman stared at me and said, "There isn't any dark-haired woman who works here. It's my shop, so it's just me. And besides, we open every day at 5:00 P.M., never earlier."

Well, think what you want, but I know I was supposed to walk in and encounter what I believe was an angel. It really gave me a lift, because the day before, I'd been obsessing about finances (yes, I do have many people to support), and after she spoke to me, I just felt that everything would be okay.

Q: When angels emit energy, why is it in a different color?

A: I think the reason for this is no more complicated than to designate their specific duties. It's similar to the idea that nurses wore white uniforms and nuns wore black habits; it was to denote their defined position. The colors emitted by angels denote their phyla and duties. Let's face it, energy has color. Oftentimes the angels' color represents not only color for healing, but for courage, help, and keeping us on track through their telepathic messages.

Q: Does believing in angels help them help us more?

A: Belief is a powerful energy. Our belief in angels helps them pierce the veil of this world from the next. Notice how children who are totally innocent are so often aware of angels because they haven't been told they can't see them.

Q: Do angels need to rest or sleep?

A: No, angels don't need to rest or sleep, nor do spirit guides, or any other entities on the Other Side. There, we each have a body, but it's a perfect, glorified body that doesn't get tired, sick, or anxious. We're all in a perfect state, or as Joseph Campbell said, "in bliss."

Q: Do angels go to a special place to worship God?

A: No, they don't need to go to any special place, the same as we don't or our Lord didn't. We can worship God in any place, anywhere, anytime, because God is everywhere. To denote a place would be to limit God's omnipotent presence. Again, God has no preferences.

Q: Do angels manifest on the Other Side?

A: Of course they do, and very visually. It's only here that they have a hard time manifesting. When we're on the Other Side or even crossing over, angels are in attendance to aid us at the first sign of trouble.

Q: Why do angels manifest sometimes to people who don't have a religious background?

A: Here again, God, like the angels or spirit guides, doesn't play favorites. Many people who have never believed will have an experience that changes their lives forever. It's just like the close-minded skeptics. (Everyone can be an open-minded skeptic.) I'm sure if an angel appeared, close-minded skeptics still wouldn't believe, but again, God has no preferences. I just feel sorry for the skeptics who don't believe in God and an afterlife or angels. It's not just faith, it's also logical that God not only exists, but has helpers who are very real and here to help us. I just feel bad that some people don't believe—not in me, but in a Higher Power. However, God bless them all anyway. They'll find out when they cross over.

There are so many other questions, but because these are the most frequently asked, I hope that they provide a deeper insight into these blessed entities that are here in service from God to help us. I truly think that believing in angels brings us closer to our own spirituality and gives us a boost to God.

Every one of us can enjoy our angels, call on them daily or whenever we think of them, and also do as I do and talk to them. The more we do so, the more aware we'll be that angels are always around us—ready and willing to give us love, courage, healing, and protection.

X

More Letters and Angel Stories

"Praise Him, all His angels; Praise Him, all His hosts!"

— Psalm 148:2

EVERYTHING WE do in this life that helps us search for spiritual truth (wherever that may be) takes us a notch upward on the ladder of expanding our spirits for God. And when all is said and done, as the phrase goes, no matter what we accomplish in life, it will never, ever be as important as seeking why we're here, who's here with us, and what it's all for. My philosophy, as many of you know already, is simple: *Love God, do good, and then shut up and go Home.* Hopefully, we'll go Home ahead of the game by exploring and learning; then truly this life will not have been in vain.

I wanted to end this book with a chapter dedicated to angel stories. As I said earlier, no single volume could hold all the stories I've received—they literally number in the thousands—so I've chosen a few of my favorites. Some are poignant, and some will simply give you chills. I hope they uplift you as much as they did me. Each letter I've been privileged to review reveals one glaring truth: The angels were there to give solace, help, healing, and protection.

The following angel stories pointedly bear up or validate the ones presented in the preceding chapters. Whether it's angels appearing in human form, or bringing help or protection, the lesson is always the same: They're here to help us and reward us with God's love and omnipotent understanding and protection.

Karen writes:

"My family has encountered many experiences with angels, but one particular incident made a huge impact on my life and really put everything into perspective for me.

"Several years ago, my kids, my very best friend, Nancy, her children, and I went to a Pizza Hut one night for dinner and fun. We stayed later than usual, not realizing that it was getting late for a school/work night. When we finally did take note of the time, we all rushed out of the restaurant and hurried to our cars. Nancy, with her children in tow, raced to her car ahead of me and my children. I was walking with my two boys, one of whom is slower than the 'average bear.'

"To get off-track for a minute, I want to explain why the younger of my boys is a little slower than the norm. Nicholas was born with a fetal-developed neuroblastoma cancer. He's been in remission for ten years now with no recurrences. The miracle of his outcome is this: At the young age of seven months, Nicholas had a cancerous tumor that was the size of a grapefruit. The tumor was removed and no further treatment was required—not even radiation or chemotherapy. The doctors were amazed by his recovery, but I knew all along that he'd be okay.

"My family really believes in the power of prayer and the magic of miracles. However, to date, we're seeing some physical/developmental challenges that Nicholas is striving hard to compromise and overcome. Neuroblastoma has left Nicholas with weak muscle tone in his lower and upper extremities, which causes his stride and mobility to be sluggish.

"This brings me back to my story—I was walking with my two boys—specifically, I was walking in the middle of my boys with Nicholas lagging behind. I was carrying our leftover pizza and wasn't paying close attention to the distance between Nicholas and me. While the rest of our group and I had already made our way past the sidewalk and onto the parking lot, I realized that Nicholas wasn't as close to me as he should have been. I glanced back to discover that he had just stepped off the sidewalk and was making his way through the parking lot.

"At that split second, I noticed a white car approaching the entrance to the parking lot at a very fast rate of speed. I yelled for Nicholas to *'Watch out!'* as I stood there in horror, waiting for an impact. The moment I yelled, everyone turned to witness Nicholas literally being launched or pushed toward us. His back arched as he catapulted through the air and landed within my arms' reach! I grabbed him as the driver of the car whizzed by without a swerve or reaction.

"The car had completely missed Nicholas without a bump or scratch. As I stood there holding Nicholas—all of us trying to catch our breaths—we just couldn't believe it. We stood in awe at what we had just witnessed and applauded Nicholas for the courageous daredevil stunt he'd just performed! Trust me when I say this: Nicholas has never moved so fast before in his ten years. And he couldn't have possibly launched his body the way he did without the help of a Presence. Nicholas just doesn't move that way or that fast, period.

"After that experience, our family now believes that not only is Nicholas full of hidden surprises, he really does have a guardian angel that protects him and watches over him. As a matter of fact, there was a Presence that used to stand in the entrance of Nicholas's bedroom. Nicholas has seen this Presence a couple of times and describes it as just a shadow with its arms folded behind its back—looking. At first it frightened my son, but I told him it was his guardian angel from Pizza Hut and not to be afraid—he was just checking in on him to make sure he was okay.

"Thank you for allowing me the opportunity to share my story with you."

This is truly a wonderful and inspiring story. The same thing more or less happened to Gina, my former daughter-in-law. She was pushing Angelia, my granddaughter, in a stroller. Gina stepped off the curb, and just as she did, she later told our entire office that unseen strong hands literally pushed her so hard that she was pressed back against the curb, only to realize that a white van was bearing down on her and Angelia. Had it not been for the somewhat violent push, they both would have been dead.

R. T. writes:

"Several years ago I was walking my dogs, as I do every day. Suddenly, I stopped in my tracks and the dogs sat down. Just behind me, I felt what seemed to be a warm wind gently coming up over my shoulders accompanied by the scent of roses. A gentle voice said, 'Now you have a guardian angel.' I've often seen angels and spirits and had numerous psychic experiences, but this was one of the most unique!"

The following story is a little long, but also beautifully represents the protection angels give over children. Cynthia writes:

"Back in 1994, I know that God sent an angel to protect my daughter, Corinne. She was six years old at that time and the light of our lives.

"My husband, Paul, and I were married seven years before she became a welcome and joyful addition to our world. He was a hands-on dad from the start, and Corinne and her father were very close. She was the apple of his eye. We enjoyed the American Dream—a good marriage, a beautiful child, and a nice home in Connecticut. Paul was a talented artist, coached Corinne's pee-wee soccer team, and worked as an instructor of sign language and with the handicapped. (Not trying to give sainthood to the man, but after 13 years of marriage, we really knew each other so well, and he was and will always be my best friend.)

"On November 17, 1994, all of our lives were changed forever. I awoke to find Paul having massive seizures as we lay in bed . . . no indication of any problems earlier that evening. He went into cardiac arrest at the age of 37. I flipped on the lights, called 911, closed my daughter's bedroom door most of the way (her room was directly across the hall about five feet away), tied up the dog, and waited for the paramedics to respond. You can well imagine the chaos that followed: sirens blasting, lights blaring, dog barking, and me screaming and crying at the top of my lungs. The EMTs were wonderful and worked hard to save a man they all knew (we lived in a small town).

"In the heat of the situation, they overturned the nightstand and sent it crashing to the ground, pulled my husband off the bed with a huge crash, and set up equipment to restart his heart, which buzzed loudly, hummed, dimmed all the lights in the house, and in general made a big racket. All this time they were yelling at him to hang on, while I screamed at them to let me get to my daughter. I wish I could tell you I felt some overwhelming choir send me peace at that juncture, but at that point it did not occur.

"As soon as I could get into the hall, as they were loading Paul into the rescue truck, I ran to check on my daughter. As I opened the door to her room (which was a bit ajar throughout this entire situation), certain that she was traumatized beyond all belief, I saw this bright light. The entire room literally *glowed*. I thought at that time that it was a reflection from all the lights outside, but the ambulance and rescue lights were all in the driveway at the opposite side of the house. This bright white light hovered over her bed, about two or three feet above the peaceful, sleeping figure of my six-year-old child, and it seemed to pulsate. Suddenly, as I walked toward it, it was gone. I kissed her and held her and realized she was sleeping very soundly. Leaving my neighbor at the house to care for her, I traveled to the hospital.

"As I lay in bed later the next night, I kept going over the past night's events. How in God's name could this child have slept through all the noise and confusion that had occurred just a few feet behind her? That is *unreal.* I then saw what I can only term as a divine vision. It wasn't a dream, since I wasn't asleep. Grief stricken, yes. Crazy . . . well, the jury on that is still out (only kidding). I'm an educated and intelligent woman. I clearly saw the figure of my daughter, sound asleep upon her bed. A bright and beautiful light began to fill the room. A wonderful, warm feeling accompanied this light. As I watched, a large robed figure appeared, floating about a foot off the floor, bright in appearance, very tall and strong, a commanding creature with light glowing all around it; the same kind of light I'd seen hovering over her bed the night before. I watched in awe as this beautiful being knelt down by the side of her bed and covered her with its wing.

"We've talked about this a great deal over the

years, and while I'm sure that many people would chalk this up to my grief-stricken state at that time and/or sleep deprivation, I truly believe with all my heart that God sent an angel to spare my daughter the pain of witnessing her father's last moments. Corinne has no memory of her 'visitor' that night. She slept soundly through the entire experience, which is amazing when you consider the small size of the hallway and the level of noise going on. It's even more amazing to me when I consider the awesome power of God."

Wendall writes:

"I don't know if this is really an angel story or not, but I had just turned 19 on November 8, 1969, and was in the military. On November 10, three other soldiers and I were walking with the traffic just inside a guard shack when we were hit by a car. I went under the vehicle, and the other three were thrown aside. I was dragged, some say 150 feet, others say 190 feet, staying conscious. When I got free of the car, I remember somer-saulting several times. I came to rest, and a lovely black woman dressed in a beautiful dress was there kneeling beside me. Even though later my survival would be in doubt, I remember feeling such love and comfort coming from her. The driver somehow got away and was never found, and to this day I have no idea who that woman was. Again, I don't know if this is an angel story, but this woman felt like one to me."

She was definitely an angel, and this also shows how angels appear in many beautiful forms to help us in our time of need. It also shows that angels come in all colors, and all are filled with love and compassion.

Mike writes:

"I'm a 49-year-old male who lives in Southern California. In October 2000, I had major heart surgery at Good Samaritan Hospital in Los Angeles. During the early evening (between 5 and 6 P.M.) the night before my scheduled surgery to replace a congenitally defective mitral valve in my heart that had left me near death, I was alone in my hospital room when a mid- to late-30ish, conservatively but tastefully attired, dark-haired, average-sized woman walked quietly into my room.

"Having been hospitalized at this time for nearly eight days preceding the actual surgery (I was gravely ill because of liver complications brought on by my heart condition), I was accustomed to people coming and going from my room at all times of the day and night for one reason or another. She walked over toward me (I was sort of half sitting up on the left edge of my bed) and said simply, 'Hello, are you having your surgery tomorrow?'

"I replied, 'Yes, that's right, tomorrow morning.'

"She asked, 'Are you concerned or nervous about the procedure?'

"Having not been told by my family or doctors about the chances of success of the surgery, I said that, no, I wasn't nervous, I just wanted them to get it done, since I wanted so badly to feel better, and the operation was the only way to relieve my misery.

"The woman, who, by the way, seemed somehow vaguely familiar to me, next asked if I was religious. I replied truthfully that, no, I was not, but that I believed in God. She then asked if I would like to pray with her. I said, 'Yes, I would.' She sat down on the other side of my bed, took my right hand in hers, placed her other hand around both of ours, closed her eyes, and began to pray.

"I remember almost nothing of the prayer except that she used the phrase 'Heavenly Father' numerous times. What I remember most vividly some 16 months after that evening was the incredible strength, firmness, and warmth (almost heat) of her hands around mine. Yet at the same time, they felt soft and somehow gentle. I've described the sensation as feeling as if I were being gripped by a gentle hockey player. She prayed for a minute or so and then stopped, released my hand, said something like 'Good luck tomorrow,' and then walked out into the corridor and was gone. At that same time, I remember feeling relaxed and at peace with everything for a short period of time. Upon reflection, I began to wonder exactly who she was. I guess I assumed she was a hospital chaplain or some such church woman who goes around visiting people about to have major operations.

"Later that evening, my wife came to visit me and I mentioned this incident to her just in passing. She said nothing at the time but later told me she thought I'd imagined the entire episode. On my admission papers, I hadn't stated any religious affiliation. She visited the hospital chaplain's office that evening after departing my room and asked the reverend on duty if he routinely sent anyone, specifically a woman, around to see pre-surgical patients. She said that he didn't unless a patient requested that he or one of his assistants (they being a Catholic priest and a rabbi) visit them before their scheduled surgery. In cases where no religious affiliation was stated, he didn't intrude into people's states of mind or disposition. He specifically told her that he was unfamiliar with any female individual within the hospital or from elsewhere who performed that sort of duty at any time.

"My wife, I think, continues to believe I hallucinated or dreamed up the entire event, but I'm just as sure that this was real and actually occurred. I can still feel the warmth and gentle strength of those hands around mine, and I remember feeling a deep connection to her while we prayed. To this day, I know I could pick her face out of a crowd of people, and I still feel that I've seen her somewhere before.

"I have no clear memory of the following, but when I was very young, my mother and grandmother tell me I had two imaginary friends or companions who were very real to me. Is it possible that's where I knew this woman from? Was this my guardian angel or spirit guide, and is it possible for me to connect with her again somehow before I die? Or is this not up to me, but rather, up to her or God? I feel certain that I will see her again when I'm ready to, and finally do, cross over."

It really doesn't matter how angels come, because they *do* come and give us solace in times of need. If we just think and keep our eyes open, I'll bet we can all remember a stranger who helped us . . . and it was probably an angel.

Kate writes:

"I have a story to share of when I was a child and met an angel. I couldn't have been more than three years old at the time, and I can remember it as if it were yesterday.

"I lived in the basement of a fourplex with my mother, two sisters, and one brother, and I remember that one evening my mother had a friend over and told us kids to go play in our room. I recall that the door was closed to the room, and for some reason none of us kids would go near it. My sisters were probably seven and eight, and my brother was two. I remember my mom getting rather annoyed with us. She got up from the living room that was just down the hall and came toward us, telling us to stop goofing around and behave.

"My next memory is of my mom opening the door to the bedroom and this very, very cold wind rushing past us. Then the bedroom got really warm. The window was closed, so being a child, I couldn't understand where the wind came from, but at the same time, being a child, I also didn't let it bother me.

"My mother herded us into a circle and had her friend join us to pray. We were raised very religiously as kids, and it always seemed that we were in church or praying at home. Anyway, the next thing I remember is my mother telling us to look for an angel.

"I remember looking all over the house but found nothing, and I was heartbroken because I really thought that I would see an angel. Just then, I checked the laundry room. I opened the door and on the dryer was sitting the most gorgeous sight I had ever seen. It scared me very much, and I must have looked absolutely petrified, because just then it spoke to me. (I say "it" because I don't know what sex it was.)

"The angel said, 'Katherine, do not be afraid. I will not hurt [or could have been *harm*] you. I will always protect you. I am your guardian angel.'

"I turned and asked my mom if she could see the angel. She said she couldn't, and I asked her why. She said it was because my heart was pure and hers wasn't, or something to that effect. Quite honestly, I don't remember if any of my siblings saw it, but I do know that they've had other encounters with other spirits, as I have, too, over the years.

"I'll never forget that experience, and I

treasure it. When I get really down, I always think of that moment and I feel like I'm being watched over. I can't really describe what the angel looked like because it was everything beautiful that you can ever imagine all in one. At the same time, it had a face but was featureless. That might not make sense to anyone else, but to me it does.

"The only thing the angel was comparable to (though very dimly) is a Greek statue with shoulder-length hair and wings that were huge and magnificent. The angel was wearing a long robe that a Greek person would have worn in ancient times, but its color was a warm gold. It was almost as if a bright, soothing light emanated from it, and this was the only color the angel had. No hair color, no skin tone, no eye color . . . just this lightness."

As I've stated many times, children are pure of heart and able to see what others many times cannot. This story also coincides with the information that angels are androgynous. Note also that the angel in this story confirms the energy emanation that angels oftentimes manifest when they appear to us, so much energy that the angel appears to be all light with no color—except the color of the energy it puts forth.

Janet writes:

"Angels around the tree . . . an image that will always stay in my mind. I was walking home from my friend's home, age five or so, and turned around and looked at my friends playing under the tree in their yard. It was like I was seeing it out of the corner of my eye. There was a beautiful female angel standing by them, watching over them. It was the kind you see in books, with large wings and beautiful clothing.

"I don't recall sharing that event until my adult years, as I felt it wasn't something to talk about with the people around me. Years later, as the situation arises, I share my experience about the guardian angel whenever it seems appropriate. This is the only time I've put this experience down in written form. Blessings to you for the opportunity to share this life experience."

This also typifies the angels' way of protecting people. I feel that we so often see them around children because kids are innocent and uncomplicated, without negativity to block them.

Susan writes:

"The week before New Year's 2001, my family and I decided to drive to West Virginia to visit my mother and let the children and grandchildren see snow for the first time. Whenever I'm going on a long trip, especially around the holidays, I ask the angels to be with us. Megan, my stepdaughter, took a picture out her window as we were driving on the interstate. When we got the developed pictures back, there were two angels with us. I keep this picture on my desk at work to remind me that my angels are always with me."

You don't know how many pictures I've seen that show either an angel outline in the sky or bright lights around the person that can' be explained away as a lens flare.

Adam writes:

"My friend's dad was driving the whole family to a vacation spot. It was very foggy outside, and visibility was at a bare minimum. He said that all of a sudden a blue light came out of nowhere from the corner of the car, showing the road more clearly. He then saw that he was off the road, about to go off a cliff. He immediately turned and got back on the road. I like this story he told me, and I believe it. This man is a very honest person, one of the very few in this world."

This story also shows that angels not only protect, but—as was related earlier in the book—they emit lights, totems, and even electrical energy.

Paula writes:

"On September 24, 2000, in Pigeon Hill, Georgia, my son, Dylan, and I decided to go hiking. Dylan had some chocolate candy with him so I put it and my camera in my fanny pack. We walked about a mile to a stream, where he played in the water, throwing rocks and walking on tree limbs. During this time, I took pictures of him playing. Then I noticed a mist rolling up the bank. My first thought was angels, but I couldn't understand why they would be there. So I looked up and down the stream; the mist was only around my son. After a few minutes, it was gone.

"Dylan played for another 30 minutes, then we decided to walk back to the car. I gave him his candy so he could have it on the way back. Dylan was walking about six feet in front of me on the edge of the trail. Then he screamed and jumped, so I rushed up to him. There was a three-foot-long cottonmouth snake in strike position looking at me. I grabbed Dylan and asked if he was okay. He told me that he'd dropped a piece of candy, which made him look down just in time to see the snake. His next step would have been on top of the snake. Then I realized why the angels were there, and I thanked them for looking after my son. The pictures I'd taken revealed the mist (angels) around Dylan that day.

"After my ordeal, I felt as if I needed to share my story with someone so I called my 84-year-old grandmother, Letitia. After I told her my story, she wanted to tell me about *her* angel story, which I want to share with you.

"Letitia fell and broke her hip several years ago. The first night home, she was awakened by a pink light over her bed. The light grew larger, and then angels in robes appeared, placing the light over her entire bed like a tent. Then they disappeared, but after that, Letitia healed very quickly from her injury. We both agreed that they were there to heal her so she could stay with us longer. Ever since this happened, Letitia has been able to see ghosts playing and angels taking care of her.

Sharing this experience with her has made our relationship even stronger."

Here again, we see not only the colored lights that angels project, but the white mist that often surrounds them.

Suzanne writes:

"I have two stories about angels, I think. I live out in the country, so I have to travel about 20 miles to get anywhere. And I like to drive a bit fast. Anyway, I was working in a grocery store, and I was straightening up the magazine rack. While there, I was greeted by many customers, and I chatted with them as I did my work. A woman whom I've never seen before or since spoke to me, and out of the blue told me to 'be careful near that church; you know the deer are hungry.' Well, I was sort of surprised at that, mostly because we'd been talking about something totally different, but I said, 'Thank you, I will be careful on the way home.'

"On the trip home that afternoon, I didn't really dwell on what that woman had said, but I went slower than the speed limit of 55. Right as I was coming around the bridge, right next to the

Chapel Hill Baptist Church, there were about eight or so deer crossing the road. I was able to stop because I wasn't going as fast as I normally would have. I was only going about 40 to 45 miles per hour. I'm sure that woman was an angel."

This was an angel giving advice and protection through a warning. Most of the time, angels come out of nowhere and then disappear. It's as if they're sent as messengers in an envelope of time to protect us.

Suzanne continued:

"The second one, I'm not sure it was an angel, but I think it was. I was going to work (in a different town, to a different job), and it was icy on the roads. I was going slowly because of the bad road conditions. I had to stop at a stoplight, but I was preparing to turn right onto a one-way street. I listen to classic rock 'n' roll, and it was near Christmas. I like to hear the carols presented traditionally, not rock style, so when this rock station played 'Joy to the World' (my favorite carol), I didn't try to turn—I was too busy staring at my radio! As I sat there, a big old tractor trailer came barreling through the red light, unable to stop because of the ice. If I'd turned when I first was able, I'd have been hit by the truck. I'm sure that was angelic intervention."

Suzanne's second story shows how God and His angels are always protecting us.

Kim writes:

"My story is one I'll never forget. It was in the summer of my seventh-grade year. I was at the beach with my friend, and we were in the ocean, jumping in the waves and having a great time. We didn't realize that the lifeguards were warning people of the undertow that was occurring. Before we knew it, we were farther out in the ocean, and the waves kept coming, one after another, and there was no one around. I was finding it hard to gasp for air between each wave, and my arms were getting very tired. Finally, I couldn't keep my head above the water any longer, and I went under. I remember my bottom hitting the ocean floor as I sat there feeling exhausted and praying over and over again for God to help me. I then realized that I wasn't struggling to get to the surface for air, and I felt like a fish, because it was as though I could breathe underwater (I had always had a fear of drowning because I thought it would be horrible not to get your next breath).

"I felt very peaceful as I prayed over and over,

then all of a sudden, I shot straight up to the surface as though I'd pushed hard from the ocean floor with my feet—but I'd been sitting on the ocean floor, not standing. I saw my friend struggling to stay afloat, and I was able to reach her hand and grab her. Then, from out in the ocean, not from the shore, came two surfers who put us on their surfboards and rode us into shore safely. The strange thing is that these two surfers were identical twins with piercing blue eyes. When we got off the boards and stood up on the shore, we turned to thank them, but they were nowhere to be found . . . not in the water or up or down the beach. I truly believe that they were angels, and it just wasn't our time to go. Because of this experience, I no longer fear death or the pain that may come with it."

This is another story of how angels take a different form. Notice, also, in this story how there were multiple angels working together, one or more to propel Kim upward, and two to rescue her and her friend.

Rose writes:

"When my daughter, Ashley, who's now 14, was 5 years old, she used to spend time in the solitude of her room. I could hear her dancing and singing from the kitchen, which was one floor down from her bedroom, and I'd think to myself, *Isn't that sweet.* One day I decided to listen in during one of her musical interludes, when my breath was taken away. As I stood silently outside her bedroom door, I could hear Ashley singing, giggling, and having a wonderful one-sided conversation. At first I thought, *Isn't that cute, she has an imaginary friend,* until I heard Ashley's beautiful little voice call out, 'It's okay, Mommy, you can come in. I was just talking with my angels. They're so funny!'

"I walked dumbfounded into her bedroom where, at the ripe old age of five, she explained to me that the angels were her friends. She told me they came to play with her all the time and if I didn't believe her, to just ask them, they were right there in the room! I was euphoric and honored to be a part of this magical moment, but told my daughter I would leave her in peace to play with her beautiful friends."

Angels have a special affinity for children because they haven't been corrupted by everyone telling them they can't see or hear them. In this case, angels were Ashley's playmates, but spirit guides have also been known to be the "imaginary playmates" of children all over the world.

This last story is a great one to finish up with, because it demonstrates and validates so many aspects of angels. Veronica writes:

"I just finished reading *The Other Side and Back,* checked out your Website, and became inspired to share a story after seeing your request for angel stories. I don't tell this story to many people.

"I was probably five or six years old, playing outside with my neighborhood friends in Mexico City, where I grew up. The street in front of our house was more of a boulevard, a wide street divided by a very wide, grassy median. We lived on a slope, which meant all traffic directly in front of our house was usually going downhill at breakneck speed. My friends lived across the street, and my mother would always implore us to be extremely careful when crossing the street to each other's houses. We were, of course, forbidden to play on the street or even the sidewalk.

"On this particular day, we were playing out a *Star Wars* scene in my neighbor's front yard. Since my brother was the supreme authority on the subject, he owned all the respective toys and assorted guns, and I volunteered to retrieve a particular model from our house. I'd learned to look both ways before crossing any street, and my parents had warned me about the dangers of this particular roadway.

"For whatever reason, on that day I either didn't look, or didn't look well enough, before crossing. I shot across the street, happy and intent on getting that toy. Next thing I knew, I saw a Volkswagen Beetle barreling toward me. I remember the instinct to take a step back toward the curb, but I was already halfway across the street. Whether the thought transformed itself into action, I don't know. I remember the sensation of being enveloped by something soft, seeing nothing but a flash of light—all in an instant. Next thing I knew and saw, I was halfway beneath the front of the car, with my hands bracing the metal bumper at my chest level. To a spectator, it might have looked as if I'd stopped the car by the bumper. I remember looking up at the front of the car and realizing I was lying on my back at the exact middle of the car, with my legs perfectly straight before me. A few seconds later, I heard and saw the footsteps of two young men rushing out of the car to get to me. I wasn't scared; instead, I remember reassuring the men that I was okay.

"I do remember the feeling of being enveloped in something soft immediately being replaced by the rather rough (in comparison) hands of the men trying to get me out from under their vehicle. I remember my mother screaming my name from our second-story window.

"The events that came after are blurred in my mind, but two things superimposed themselves on my memory of the remainder of that day: the absolute certainty that I'd been touched by something pure and holy (the feeling stayed with me for several days afterwards, like an afterglow), and extreme gratitude that I was intact—not a scratch, bump, or bruise from an event that by all accounts should have resulted in severely broken legs at best, and death at worst. There's no other explanation for the way I was positioned beneath the car; for the lack of bruises and injury; and for the soft, enveloping sensation I experienced. I'm certain that that miracle was the work of my angel."

This is a prime example of the angels' miraculous ability to protect and defend us. Again, it makes me crazy when I hear some people ask, "What do angels do, anyway?" If we just think back, we'll all remember how many

near-disasters were averted by the swift and loving intervention of angels.

Epilogue

PERHAPS BECAUSE of all these beautiful, true, and uplifting stories about angels, a wonderful realization began to dawn on me as I was writing this book. I'm convinced, without being humble, that God, as well as our guides and angels, infuse us all with profound truths. If we keep ourselves open, their message will just ticker-tape through our minds.

People say to me more often than I could ever count: "The more I'm aware and know, the more psychic I'm becoming." I've never understood why we try to separate the two. The more our minds, hearts, and souls reach out to God, the more information comes in. I've always believed that, using modern verbiage, we were all born with a cell phone, or two paper cups with a string, or the ability to get smoke signals from God; but we forgot how to use this ability, had it drummed out of us, or just dropped it completely. Not just "religionistically" (notice that this is different from religion), but because life crowded in and pushed divine reciprocation out.

This simple truth came to me as a result of thinking about that age-old, often-asked question: *Where is my soul mate, where is my twin soul, or where is the one person who will make me whole?* We forget that there are many to love, including those seen and unseen: our past loved ones, our guides, our angels, and last but never, ever least, God. I'm convinced that the reason humankind is always looking for love and why life often doesn't seem complete is because down here on the Earth plane, we're separated, or so we sometimes feel, from the Ultimate, which is not just the Other Side, but God's omnipresent love.

Love is truly the answer to everything. To be godlike is to be in a state of loving, not just always *wanting* to be loved. The angels show us this concept in its truest form. Yes, we have love here, but not like over on the Other Side, which is Home. So, we vainly look for that perfection in everyone and everything here; and when we feel that it betrays us, we become despondent. All humankind is filled with errors and mistakes, but that doesn't take away from Our Ultimate Divinity, because coming from God, we have perfect genetics.

Once we embrace that we're here, as I often say, on a bad camping trip, and that we can get through it with God, our ultimate Love, and all the heavenly hosts that attend us, life takes on a richer, fuller meaning. This is never to discredit the idea that we should have a partner; but until we incorporate God and His beloved minions, we seem to be doomed for failure and mistakes. Someday we will all be reunited with our loved ones . . . and our blessed Creator and our beautiful angels will help us get there.

God love you, I do,

— **Sylvia**

P.S. Always keep an angel on your shoulder, or for that matter, on both shoulders—or anywhere else you can think of. Even if you don't ask, your angels will come anyway, because they're an extension of God's Ultimate Love for us all.

About the Author

Millions of people have witnessed **Sylvia Browne's** incredible psychic powers on TV shows such as **Montel, Larry King Live, Entertainment Tonight,** and **Unsolved Mysteries,** and she has been profiled in **Cosmopolitan** and **People** magazines and other national media. Sylvia is the author of numerous books and audios; is president of the Sylvia Browne Corporation; and is the founder of her church, the Society of Novus Spiritus, located in Campbell, California. Please contact Sylvia at: **www.sylvia.org,** or call **408-379-7070** for further information about her work.

About the Artist

Christina Simonds is on the staff at Sylvia Browne's office, and is an ordained minister of the Society of Novus Spiritus. She's an illustrator who sees her work as a means to convey the Gnostic Christian philosophy through symbolism within her art. To purchase reprints of the drawings in this book, please visit her Website at: www.angelart–cs.com.

Hay House Titles of Related Interest

BOOKS

The Angel by My Side: *The True Story of a Dog Who Saved a Man . . . and a Man Who Saved a Dog* by Mike Lingenfelter and David Frei

Archangels & Ascended Masters: *A Guide to Working and Healing with Divinities and Deities,* by Doreen Virtue, Ph.D.

*Crossing Over: *The Stories Behind the Stories,* by John Edward

Earth Angels: *A Pocket Guide for Incarnated Angels, Elementals, Starpeople, Walk-Ins, and Wizards,* by Doreen Virtue, Ph.D.

Healing with the Angels: *How the Angels Can Assist You in Every Area of Your Life,* by Doreen Virtue, Ph.D.

The Indigo Children: *The New Kids Have Arrived,* by Lee Carroll and Jan Tober

Sacred Ceremony: *How to Create Ceremonies for Healing, Transitions, and Celebrations*
by Steven D. Farmer, Ph.D.

Visionseeker: *Shared Wisdom from the Place of Refuge,*
by Hank Wesselman, Ph.D.

AUDIO PROGRAMS

Angels! Angels! Angels! by Denise Linn

Invocation of the Angels, by Joan Borysenko, Ph.D.

Understanding Your Angels and Meeting Your Guides,
by John Edward

All of the above are available at your
local bookstore, or may be ordered by visiting:

Hay House USA: **www.hayhouse.com**
Hay House Australia: **www.hayhouse.com.au**
Hay House UK: **www.hayhouse.co.uk**
Hay House South Africa: **orders@psdprom.co.za**

*Crossing Over is published by Princess Books and
distributed by Hay House

Notes

Notes

Notes

Notes

Notes

Notes

We hope you enjoyed this Hay House book. If you would like to receive a free catalog featuring additional Hay House books and products, or if you would like information about the Hay Foundation, please contact:

Hay House, Inc.
P.O. Box 5100
Carlsbad, CA 92018-5100

(760) 431-7695 or (800) 654-5126
(760) 431-6948 (fax) or (800) 650-5115 (fax)
www.hayhouse.com

Published and distributed in Australia by:
Hay House Australia Pty. Ltd. • 18/36 Ralph St. • Alexandria NSW 2015
Phone: 612-9669-4299 • *Fax:* 612-9669-4144 • www.hayhouse.com.au

Published and distributed in the United Kingdom by:
Hay House UK, Ltd. • Unit 62, Canalot Studios
222 Kensal Rd., London W10 5BN
Phone: 44-20-8962-1230 • *Fax:* 44-20-8962-1239
www.hayhouse.co.uk

Published and distributed in the Republic of South Africa by:
Hay House SA (Pty), Ltd., P.O. Box 990, Witkoppen 2068
Phone/Fax: 2711-7012233 • orders@psdprom.co.za

Distributed in Canada by:
Raincoast • 9050 Shaughnessy St., Vancouver, B.C. V6P 6E5
Phone: (604) 323-7100 • *Fax:* (604) 323-2600

THIS IS THE NEWSLETTER YOU'VE BEEN WAITING FOR . . .

Find out
SYLVIA BROWNE'S
secrets for developing
your psychic powers!

Order your subscription today to the *Sylvia Browne Newsletter*, and receive an exclusive lecture tape from Psychic Sylvia Browne—absolutely **FREE!**

Now is your chance to hear from your favorite author and psychic Sylvia Browne —six times a year—in the pages of this remarkable newsletter!

As a subscriber to the newsletter, you'll learn inside information directly from Sylvia Browne. You'll find out how to **connect with your angels,** learn about the **Other Side,** and get Sylvia's latest **predictions,** as well as information on how to **get and stay healthy.**

You'll be the first to hear about **the latest psychic discoveries** of Sylvia or

her psychic son, **Chris Dufresne.** Also, your subscription allows you to **write to Sylvia** whenever you want, and as often as you like—and one of your questions may be featured in an upcoming newsletter along with Sylvia's answer.

Send for your Subscription and FREE lecture tape today!

IN A RUSH? Call **800-654-5126,** or fax postcard to **800-650-5115!**
www.hayhouse.com

Fold along dotted line.

Exclusive Sylvia Browne Lecture Tape—FREE!
With one-year subscription to *The Sylvia Browne Newsletter*

❏ **YES!** Enter my one-year subscription to *Sylvia Browne's Newsletter* today at the low rate of $19.95, and send my FREE lecture tape immediately. I understand that I may cancel this subscription at any time for a full refund for remaining newsletters, and that the free gift is mine to keep.

Name_____

Address_____

City, State, Zip_____

Phone _____

E-mail _____
(I authorize Hay House to send me information via e-mail)

Method of Payment:

❏ Visa   ❏ MasterCard   ❏ AmEx   ❏ Discover   ❏ Check or Money Order

Card No._____ Exp. Date_____

Signature_____

Please tape closed. Do not staple.

Exclusive
SYLVIA BROWNE
Lecture Tape—FREE!

With one-year subscription

Fold along dotted line.